Jesus' Prayer:
The Christian Story

Notes of an Explorer

Bert Cameron

Jesus' Prayer: The Christian Story—Notes of an Explorer
Copyright © 2024 Eugene C. Cameron

All rights reserved. No part of this publication may be reproduced, stored in a retrieval system, or transmitted, in any form or by any means, electronic, mechanical, photocopying, recording or otherwise, without the prior written permission of the author, except in the case of brief quotations embodied in critical articles and reviews.

ISBN: 978-1-57383-604-3

Scriptures taken from the Holy Bible, New International Version®, NIV®. Copyright © 1973, 1978, 1984, 2011 by Biblica, Inc.™ Used by permission of Zondervan. All rights reserved worldwide. www.zondervan.com The "NIV" and "New International Version" are trademarks registered in the United States Patent and Trademark Office by Biblica, Inc.™

The cover design depicts a tour boat on the Sea of Galilee. It is believed that "Jesus' Prayer" was taught to his disciples at a sight overlooking the lake. The picture has personal significance because, in 1999, we sailed on such a boat when visiting the Holy Land with a group of friends.

Contents

Preface	vii
Acknowledgements	ix
1. Introduction	1

Part One: God's Character, Kingdom, and Will

2. The Opening: "Our Father in Heaven"	9
3. The First Petition: "May Your Name Be Hallowed"	15
4. The Second Petition: "Your Kingdom Come"	22
5. The Third Petition: "Your Will Be Done on Earth as It Is in Heaven"	55

Part Two: Our Physical and Spiritual Needs

6. The Fourth Petition: "Give Us Today Our Daily Bread"	77
7. The Fifth Petition: "Forgive Us Our Debts, as We Also Have Forgiven Our Debtors"	81
8. The Sixth Petition: "Lead Us Not into Temptation"	89
9. The Seventh Petition: "Deliver Us from the Evil One"	93
10. Matthew's Closing (KJV): "For Thine Is the Kingdom, and the Power, and the Glory, For Ever. Amen."	97

Afterword	99
Appendix 1: The Creeds	101
Appendix 2: The Story of Jesus' Life	103
Appendix 3: The Ten Commandments	117
References and Notes	119

For our sons,
Mark, Richard, and Gordon,
and for their families.

Preface

The Christian Bible contains a "grand story" about the meaning of life and the best way to live it. We all live within a personal and cultural story, sometimes called a "worldview" or "framework of understanding." The story within which we live shapes how we live. The philosopher Alasdair MacIntyre has written, "I can only answer the question 'What am I to do' if I can answer the prior question, 'Of what story or stories do I find myself a part.'"[1] Accepting and becoming part of the Christian story has radical implications for the questions, what should I do, and how shall I live?

The idea of writing *Notes of an Explorer* arose a number of years ago while I was reading the works of the scientist and philosopher Michael Polanyi. I was drawn to Polanyi's vision that human beings constitute what he calls a "Society of Explorers—a society in which each human being is given a calling to be an active center pursuing truth with universal intent. . . . The acceptance of this calling places upon us the burden and the opportunity of responsibility for seeking the truth and stating our findings."[2]

In response to that perceived calling to state "my truth," I envisaged writing about my understanding of the Christian faith. Though I did not undertake the project at the time, the idea did not die. Many years later, I have completed this writing as an attempt to explore and document my understanding of the Christian story by focusing on the recorded teachings of Jesus, explored through the framework of the Lord's Prayer.

For whom are these Notes written? First, they are a personal initiative. After many years of being a Christian, the opportunity to collate and reflect on the unique words of Jesus has been a very fulfilling experience. In this project, the value may have been more in the process than the product.

Who else might be interested in reading this? Perhaps those who, like me, will appreciate reviewing the ground of their faith through the teachings of Jesus and as a guide to more in-depth study of the Christian story. These Notes may also be useful for some who are interested in the Christian faith and wish to hear what Jesus, himself, had to say.

Acknowledgements

I am very grateful to my wife, Sonja, for reading and editing many iterations of these *Notes*. My brother, David, and my son, Mark, read early drafts and made helpful suggestions.

I am particularly indebted to my friend Wally Eggert for his enthusiastic support of this project and for making many significant recommendations.

Members of the Regent College community have provided very important advice, including Julie Lane-Gay, Stephen Gomez, Bill Reimer, and Richard Thompson. Iain Provan planted the seed for this book focused on the Christian story, in a seminar I attended.

I must recognize the many faithful teachers I have encountered in the context of family, church, parachurch, and Christian educational institutions.

Bethany Murphy has been a patient and skilful editor, and Robert Hand helped with the interior and cover design and distribution arrangements.

1

Introduction

In the past, the Christian story had a major influence on the development of the social norms and structures of Western society.[3] However, in today's ethos, there has been a marked decline in knowledge about Christian Scriptures and beliefs. Further, there is widespread cynicism because of the social evils that have been committed in the context of the Christian church. The question may be asked, Does the Christian story and the teaching of Jesus continue to have relevance? The answer to that question is very personal, but it cannot possibly be answered if Jesus' teachings are not heard.

What Is the Christian Story?

In the fourth century CE, the basic elements of the Christian story were codified into creeds by the ancient church. The Apostle's Creed and the Nicene Creed (appendix 1) are the most widely accepted summaries of Christian beliefs and continue to be recited in churches today. However, the Christian story, as summarized in the creeds, is merely a historical artifact unless it is understood to be personally meaningful.

I have come to appreciate that the Christian story is best told through the teachings of Jesus himself. It is essential for anyone who seeks an understanding of God to consider his words. Jesus claimed,

> Therefore, everyone who *hears these words of mine and puts them into practice* is like a wise man who built his house on the rock. (Matt. 7:24)
>
> I am the way and the truth and the life. *No one comes to the Father except through me.* (John 14:6)

What else did Jesus teach? In this book I intend to provide an overview of what Jesus said. Notes of an Explorer is based on the belief that, as Jesus claimed, his teachings offer the foundation for a fulfilled life in relationship with God.

Jesus' Prayer and the Christian Story

Jesus himself provided a remarkably cogent summary of the Christian story in what is called the Lord's Prayer, recorded in the gospels of Matthew and Luke. This understanding has been recognized in the Catechism of the Catholic Church. The Lord's Prayer is "truly a summary of the whole gospel."[4]

The most complete version is found in Jesus' Sermon on the Mount (Matthew 5–7). When Jesus' disciples asked him to teach them to pray, he gave them a model prayer that has become one of the best-known portions of the Bible.

The opening and seven petitions of this prayer identify the vital elements and the relational nature of the Christian story. In *Notes of an Explorer*, the words of Jesus' prayer are used as a framework for telling the story. He says,

> This, then, is how you should pray:
> Our Father in heaven,
> hallowed be your name,
> your kingdom come,
> your will be done,
> on earth as it is in heaven.
> Give us today our daily bread.
> And forgive us our debts,
> as we also have forgiven our debtors.
> And lead us not into temptation,
> but deliver us from the evil one. (Matt. 6:8–13)

This prayer is recited weekly in many churches and is the subject of countless sermons and books. Darrell Johnson named his book on this "brilliant" prayer *Fifty-Seven Words That Changed the World*.[5] As previously stated, the petitions of this prayer address the major themes of Jesus' teaching and provide a framework to explore what he said.

Jesus' Words Tell the Christian Story

The earliest Christians did not have access to the written words of Jesus. In the early decades after he left the earth, the community of his followers expanded widely, based on verbal testimony about Jesus' life and teachings, supported by letters that were written to early churches by his apostles. Those letters, now compiled in the New Testament, did not quote Jesus directly, but they did communicate the full essence of his message. However, within seventy years of Jesus' lifetime, eyewitness accounts of his life and teachings were gathered into the Four Gospels of the New Testament, Matthew, Mark, Luke, and John.[6]

The fact that Jesus' words have reached us today is an incredible story. The common language of Palestine in Jesus' time was Aramaic, and most of Jesus' original sayings would have been in that language. His words were translated into Greek and recorded in the Gospels, sourced from collected eyewitness material. These Gospels were written for the Greek speaking churches in the Roman Empire. By the early third century, the four Gospels were widely accepted as foundational Christian documents. In appendix 3, "The Story of Jesus' Life," the development and character of the Gospels are more fully discussed.

Over the past two thousand years, Jesus' words have been translated multiple times into most of the world's languages. The translation used in these *Notes* is the New International Version unless otherwise noted. The locations of Jesus' words in the Gospels are referenced to encourage further study of the larger context. In addition, each of the biblical quotations has a capital letter superscript [A, B, etc.] so that the "when and where" of these quotations may be identified by using appendix 3.

The selection of Jesus' teachings, the attending commentary, and the quotations reflect my experience and study of the Christian story in the context of church, parachurch, and Christian educational organizations.

The words of Jesus are inextricably linked to the writings of the Hebrew Scriptures. Much of Jesus' teaching includes direct quotations from, or allusion to, Old Testament writings. The Christian story, as told by Jesus and his early followers, is a reinterpretation of the moral instruction, prophecy, and poetry of the Old Testament. Jesus taught his disciples, "Everything must be fulfilled that is written about me in the Law of Moses, the Prophets and the Psalms" (Luke 24:44). Thus, the Hebrew Scriptures have been grounding documents in the teachings of Jesus and the life of the Christian church.

Part One

God's Character, Kingdom, and Will

2

The Opening: "Our Father in Heaven"

The start of Jesus' prayer, "Our Father in heaven," addresses the God whom he came to represent and to whom his followers were to pray. These few words describe God as *creator*, as *personal*, and as *transcendent and moral*.

The Creator God

The word "father" implies a person who generates and provides. Jesus taught that God the Father was the creator and sustainer of the universe and the provider of human physical needs. This understanding was made clear by Jesus' words:

> Your *Father in heaven* . . . causes *his* sun to rise on the evil and the good, and sends rain on the righteous and the unrighteous. (Matt. 5:45^E)

Jesus taught that the sun, the weather, and righteous and unrighteous human beings are God's creation and under God's care. If a person does not accept the possibility of a creator God, they cannot hear the message of Jesus beyond moral platitudes. Therefore, as this overview of Jesus' teaching begins, it may be beneficial to briefly address the issue of belief in God.

There have been philosophic atheists since ancient times, but the scientific discoveries and technological advances of the modern era seemed to provide a plausible alternative to belief in a creator God. In recent years, many popular books promoting this atheistic point of view have been written by such authors as Richard Dawkins, Daniel Dennett, Sam Harris, and Christopher Hitchens.[7] These authors assert that it is their imperative to eliminate the error of religious belief on moral and rational grounds with the intention of building a better society. The result, thus far, has not been promising.

It is also a reality, as described by the Nobel Prize winner Peter Medawar,[8] that by its very nature science cannot answer the ultimate questions about the origin and purpose of existence. Ultimately, "being an atheist" is a personal choice that an individual may hold for a number of reasons. However, it must be emphasized that the question about the existence of *the Father* cannot be answered through empirical enquiry.

Human beings possess intuition of a higher intelligent power. Even the atheist Richard Dawkins stated that *it takes courage not to believe.*[9] Belief in the Father is not irrational, but neither can it be established by reasoned argument. Science gives knowledge about an amazing universe, both in scope and complexity. In the Christian story, understanding, subduing, and ruling over nature are divinely mandated human projects (Genesis 1 and 2). Thus, scientific pursuit is encompassed in the Christian story and, in fact, thrived in the context of Western Christian culture. However, the main thrust of the Christian story is about human relationship with the person of God, through the life and teaching of Jesus.

Genesis, the first book of the Bible, begins with a story of God's creative activity. Christian values flow from the belief that nature, including human nature, is not the ultimate reality. In the Christian story, God is revealed as the creator, and the human being is the epitome of his creation. Humans are truly remarkable creatures, described in the Bible as being "made in the image of God", (Gen. 1:27) having minds that perceive, understand, create, and choose; they are given the freedom even to reject the will of the creator.

In summary: atheism holds little promise, empirical science does not preclude belief in God, and physical wonder, beauty, and human capacity imply a higher power. The Christian story reveals God to be a relational being who created humankind in his own image, and in order to enter relationship with Him.

The Personal God

Jesus taught that a personal relationship between God and humankind is possible. In everyday usage, the words "our father" imply a very close family relationship. Jesus himself demonstrated such a relationship with the Father in heaven. It was because the disciples observed Jesus in prayer with the Father that they asked him to teach them to pray. On many occasions, Jesus described his intimate relationship with God. When the Jewish leaders questioned Jesus' authority, he responded,

> Very truly I tell you, the Son can do nothing by himself; he can do only what he sees his Father doing, because whatever the Father does the Son also does. *For the Father loves the Son and shows him all he does.* (John 5:19–20[F])

It is very significant that this prayer was addressed to "*our* Father." By doing so, Jesus included his followers in that personal relationship. Immediately before Jesus taught his disciples about what to pray, he instructed them about how to pray. He described the close relationship with God that Jesus expected his followers to experience.

> But when you pray, go into your room, close the door and pray to *your Father*, who is unseen. Then *your Father*, who sees what is done in secret, will reward you. And when you pray, do not keep on babbling like pagans, for they think they will be heard because of their many words. Do not be like them, for *your Father knows what you need before you ask him.* (Matt. 6:6–8[E])

The very act of prayer itself is the entrée into living the Christian story. Blaise Pascal wrote that God has established prayer "to communicate to His creatures the dignity of causality."[10] Jesus taught the disciples to interact with the Father as a person who knows them and responds to what they need. All of Jesus' teaching is to be received, not as impersonal directives, but as communication from a caring God. Jesus said,

> Ask and it will be given to you; seek and you will find; knock and the door will be opened to you. For every-

one who asks receives; the one who seeks finds; and to the one who knocks, the door will be opened. Which of you, if your son asks for bread, will give him a stone? Or if he asks for a fish, will give him a snake? If you, then, though you are evil, know how to give good gifts to your children, how much more will your Father in heaven give good gifts to those who ask him! (Matt. 7:7–11^E)

The introductory words "our Father" emphasize the communal relationship of Jesus' followers. The entire prayer is not only about "me" but is also about "us." Every time this prayer is repeated, it is a reminder of our relationship to all the others in God's family.

The Transcendent and Moral God

Addressing God as "our Father *in heaven*" links with the third petition in this prayer, "your will be done on earth *as it is in heaven*," indicating that God's moral domain is far greater than this earth. The word "heaven" denotes a conceptual location where God's moral will is fully realized; where the fullness of God is expressed. The Jews of the time used the term "heaven" as a synonym for "God." This understanding is evident in the book of Matthew where the "kingdom of God" is termed "the kingdom of heaven."

The belief in *one* moral and powerful God, creator beyond nature, was one of the most significant contributions of the Jewish religion. As the Christian story began, Jesus taught that God the Father was the powerful creator and sustainer of the universe, the God who relates personally with his human creation, and the moral force who underlies reality and ultimately controls human destiny.

Jesus began his prayer by addressing "our Father in heaven," teaching us that God is the creating, personal, and transcendent and moral God.

3

The First Petition: "May Your Name Be Hallowed"

The first three petitions focus on the nature, rule, and will of God. In this first petition, Jesus begins with the *name* of God. In the Bible, "name" was used to denote the character or personality of an individual. Everything in this prayer flows from Jesus' revelation of the loving and just personhood of God. Human beings are called to "hallow," to honor or revere, God's compassionate character, which is the basis for a personal relationship with God.

Honoring God's name is more than an attitude; it is behavior that reflects the character of God into society. Jesus taught that God's character is "glorified" among people through the loving and righteous actions of his followers.

> In the same way, let your light shine before others, that *they may see your good deeds* and *glorify your Father in heaven.* (Matt. 5:16^E)

A difficult problem, throughout Christian history, has been the dishonor brought upon the character of God by the significant "bad deeds" committed by those claiming to be Jesus' followers. This very serious issue will be discussed later.

Perhaps Jesus' most lucid depiction of the loving character of God is presented in the parable of the prodigal son (Luke 15:11–32[H]). For context, the story was told to an audience of "tax collectors and sinners," watched by disapproving "pharisees and teachers of the law." The story has much nuance, but in the simplest terms, a son took his inheritance and forsook his father's household. This son later became destitute, returned to the father, and begged to become like a hired servant. The remarkable part of the story is Jesus' description of the gracious response of the father:

> But while he [the son] was still a long way off, his father saw him and was filled with compassion for him; he ran to his son, threw his arms around him and kissed him. The son said to him, "Father, I have sinned against heaven and against you. I am no longer worthy to be called your son." But the father said to his servants, "Quick! Bring the best robe and put it on him. Put a ring on his finger and sandals on his feet. Bring the fattened calf and kill it. Let's have a feast and celebrate. For this son of mine was dead and is alive again; he was lost and is found." (Luke 15:20–24[H])

But there was another son who was out working on the property. He heard the celebration of his brother's return and refused to participate.

> The older brother became angry and refused to go in. So his father went out and pleaded with him. But he

answered his father, "Look! All these years I've been slaving for you and never disobeyed your orders. Yet you never gave me even a young goat so I could celebrate with my friends. But when this son of yours who has squandered your property with prostitutes comes home, you kill the fattened calf for him!"

"My son" the father said, "you are always with me, and everything I have is yours. But we had to celebrate and be glad, because this brother of yours was dead and is alive again; he was lost and is found." (Luke 15:25-32[H])

In this parable, Jesus portrayed the depth and breadth of God's amazing love, reaching from the repentant sinner to the self-righteous and cynical.

Jesus made many references to the loving nature of the Father, but his most astonishing claim was that *he himself* was the full demonstration of God's moral character. In discussion with his disciples, Jesus said,

If you really know me, you will know my Father as well. From now on, you do know him and have seen him. Philip said, "Lord, show us the Father and that will be enough for us."

Jesus answered: "Don't you know me, Philip, even after I have been among you such a long time? *Anyone who has seen me has seen the Father.* How can you say, 'Show us the Father'? Don't you believe that I am in the Father, and that the Father is in me? The words I say to you I do not speak on my own authority. Rather, *it is the Father, living in me, who is doing his work.* Believe me when I say that I am in the Father and the Father is in me." (John 14:7–11[I])

The above statement is the crux of the Christian story, that the loving personhood of God was fully displayed in the life and teaching of Jesus.

Jesus taught that the love of God would bring freedom and healing into society through him. He took on this Messianic persona in his first recorded teaching given in the synagogue of his home village:

> He went to Nazareth, where he had been brought up, and on the Sabbath day he went into the synagogue, as was his custom. He stood up to read, and the scroll of the prophet Isaiah was handed to him. Unrolling it, he found the place where it is written:
> "The Spirit of the Lord is on me,
> because he has anointed me
> to proclaim good news to the *poor*.
> He has sent me to proclaim freedom for the *prisoners*
> and recovery of sight for the *blind*,
> to set the *oppressed* free,
> to proclaim the year of the Lord's favor."
> Then he rolled up the scroll, gave it back to the attendant and sat down. The eyes of everyone in the synagogue were fastened on him. He began by saying to them, "Today *this scripture is fulfilled in your hearing.*" (Luke 4:16–20[E])

Initially, after Jesus said these words, his hearers were "amazed by [his] gracious words" (v. 22). Later, however, they became furious when he continued by referring to the Hebrew prophets Elijah and Elisha, *who served Gentiles and not exclusively Jews* (vv. 24–27). Jesus declared that God's love, and his service, were *for people of all nations*.

Jesus taught that the Father's love involved bringing justice *and the judgment* of evil. Jesus was scathingly critical of the Jewish leaders of his time for using the temple worship of God to make personal gain at the expense of those who came to worship. On one occasion, Jesus violently overturned the tables of the money changers in the temple who were impeding people from access to worship. He declared,

> It is written, . . . "My house will be called a house of prayer," but you are making it "a den of robbers." (Matt. 21:13[I]; quoting Isa. 56:7 and Jer. 7:11)

When talking about abuse of children, Jesus pronounced severe judgment.

> And whoever welcomes one such child in my name welcomes me. If anyone causes one of these little ones—those who believe in me—to stumble, it would be better for them to have a large millstone hung around their neck and to be drowned in the depths of the sea. (Matt. 18:5–6[H])

The fact that the Father's love must include judgment of evil has significant implications, since none of us naturally live according to God's moral standards regarding others. Therefore, in order to establish a relationship with us, *God's love must also include forgiveness.* As previously noted, the reality of God's forgiving love was dramatically portrayed in the story of the prodigal son, when the father ran out unceremoniously to greet his returning rebellious son. God's forgiving character is even more poignantly demonstrated through Jesus when he was dying on the cross. He cried out for God to forgive those who were torturing him:

> Father, forgive them, for they do not know what they are doing. (Matt. 23:34[1])

Forgiveness and salvation are central themes in the teaching of Jesus. Before he was born, he was given his name, "Jesus," to indicate that he was a savior. Joseph, his earthly father, was instructed by an angel,

> She [Mary] will bear a son, and you shall call his name *Jesus*, for he will *save his people from their sins.* (Matt. 1:21[A])

Jesus' earthly name, "Yah"-"shuah," "God"-"to save," was in itself an expression of the loving and forgiving character of the Father.

The fact that all humans are sinful and need forgiveness was a fundamental postulate of Judaism and at the root of the Judaic sacrificial system. For Jesus, human sinfulness and the consequent broken relationship with the Father was an existential problem. Jesus did not discuss the ultimate origin of evil; his focus was upon himself as the remedy for human sin.

In the Christian story, the loving character of the Father, whom we are called to revere, is *fully revealed* in Jesus who *heals and restores* those who acknowledge their need and *judges* those who would harm others. Our confidence to proceed with the further petitions of the Lord's Prayer is grounded in our belief in the loving, just, and forgiving character (name) of God and of his Son, Jesus Christ.

4

The Second Petition: "Your Kingdom Come"

The first petition focused on the character of God the Father and the appropriate human response. In this second petition, Jesus directed attention to who he was and what he came to do. In the Christian story, *Jesus is the king, and his followers are subjects in God's kingdom on earth.*

Much of Jesus teaching concerned God's coming and future kingdom. Therefore, in this chapter Jesus' words are divided to reflect the many facets this topic: the arrival, nature, foundation, empowerment by the presence of God's Spirit, the membership, communal life, and the fulfilment of God's kingdom. The chapter concludes with some of Jesus' parables about the kingdom.

The Arrival of the Kingdom

In the Gospel of Matthew, Jesus' kingly status was proclaimed at the time of his birth. It is recorded that oriental Magi came to Jerusalem, looking for him and asking,

> Where is the one who has been born *king of the Jews*? (Matt. 2:2[B])

In Jewish society at the time of Jesus, there was a strong expectation that the "kingdom of God" would soon become reality for Israel. This kingdom was believed to be established by the Messiah who would restore national power to the oppressed nation.

The prophet and forerunner of Jesus, John the Baptist, was drawing crowds and proclaiming the imminent arrival of God's kingdom. He was

> preaching in the wilderness of Judea and saying, "Repent, for the *kingdom of heaven* has come near." (Matt. 3:1–2^C)

The first recorded words of Jesus in the Gospel of Mark declare the arrival of God's kingdom.

> *The time has come*, he said. *The kingdom of God has come near*. Repent and believe the good news! (Mark 1:15^E)

Because of Jesus' claim, the religious rulers asked Jesus when the kingdom of God was coming.

> He answered them and said, "The kingdom of God is not coming with signs to be observed; nor will they say, 'Look, here it is!' or 'There it is!' *For behold, the kingdom of God is in your midst*." (Luke 17:20–21^H TNIV)

Clearly, Jesus claimed that God's kingdom had come with his presence. This message was *the good news* ("the gospel"). However, this was not to be a national kingdom, and Jesus was not the kind of Messiah that the Jewish people expected.

The Jewish Messiah (or "Christ" in Greek translation) was believed to be a liberator with the characteristics of a king and priest: he was to be born in the line of King David and would unify the nation, free them from the dominion of Rome, and establish a reign of peace. The teachings of Jesus and the writings of his early followers radically transformed this understanding.

The Gospel of John was selective and particularly focused on affirming the Messianic identity of Jesus. John wrote,

> But *these are written that you may believe that Jesus is the Messiah, the Son of God,* and that by believing you may have life in his name. (John 20:31^L)

One of the clearest statements Jesus made about himself occurred when he was at the trial before his crucifixion.

> Again, the high priest asked him, "Are you the Messiah, the Son of the Blessed One?" "*I am,*" said Jesus. "*And you will see the Son of Man sitting at the right hand of the Mighty One and coming on the clouds of heaven.*" The high priest tore his clothes. "Why do we need any more witnesses?" he asked. "You have heard the blasphemy. What do you think?" They all condemned him as worthy of death. (Mark 14:61–64^J)

The grand prologue of the Gospel of John (1:1–18) describes the belief of the early Christians that Jesus was the eternal and creating God, speaking God's word into the world, bringing light into darkness, and giving spiritual life to humankind through relationship with God. John wrote,

> In the beginning was the Word, and the Word was with God, and the Word was God. . . . In him was life and that life was the light of all mankind. . . . [He was] the true light that gives light to everyone. (John 1:1, 4, 9ᴴ)

John recorded eight encounters where Jesus taught about his supreme role. In the Old Testament, God named himself "I Aᴍ" (Exodus 3). In John's Gospel, Jesus used the "I am" designation to claim that he was the pre-existent Son of God and provider of spiritual life and light, not only for the Jews but for all humankind.

- I tell you the truth . . . before Abraham was born, *I am!* (8:58ᴴ)
- While I am in the world, *I am the light of the world.* (9:5ᴴ)
- *I am the bread of life.* Whoever comes to me will never go hungry. (6:35ᴳ)
- *I am the light of the world.* Whoever follows me will never walk in darkness. (8:12ᴴ)
- *I am the gate;* whoever enters through me will be saved. (10:9ᴴ)
- *I am the good shepherd.* The good shepherd lays down his life for the sheep. (10:11, see also v. 14ᴴ)
- *I am the resurrection and the life.* . . . The one who believes in me will live, even though they die. (11:25ᴴ)

- *I am the way and the truth and the life.* No one comes to the Father except through me. (14:6¹)
- *I am the vine;* you are the branches. (15:5; see also v. 1I)

It is of note that many of these *I am* statements are focused on the very personal relationship between Jesus and his followers. Jesus promised to provide nourishment, give guidance, and be the way to God. He likened himself to a vine from which the branches (his followers) receive life. Jesus taught that relationship with him was the way to a personal relationship with God. As will be discussed further, after his resurrection, this relationship comes to his followers through God's Spirit, often referred to in the apostolic writings as "the Spirit of Christ." (Rom. 8:9, 1 Pet. 1:11)

In the Christian story, God's kingdom is founded on the teaching of Jesus about himself, the events of his life, and the nature of reality. The implications of the story are so profound for individuals and society that the issue of the *truth* of Jesus' teaching is critical. Jesus stated, "I am the way and *the truth* and the life." (John 14:6¹). Jesus' claim, that what he taught about God and humankind was "true" (represented reality), is not empirically testable. It is a claim that can only be tested personally. Jesus' followers, the apostolic writers, defended the truth of the gospel as experienced in their lives, even though they received strong opposition, often to the point of death. The truth of Jesus' teaching is much challenged in our world today. As will be further discussed, Jesus taught that his followers would be confirmed in the truth of his teaching by the Spirit of God:

> But when he, the Spirit of truth, comes, he will guide you into all the truth. (John 16:13[1])

The grand theme of the Christian story is that Jesus was the Messiah ("Christ"), the Son of God; God in person came to earth to bring reconciliation and personal relationship with God and to establish a new spiritual kingdom.

The Nature of God's Kingdom on Earth

When Jesus was on trial before the Roman procurator Pontius Pilate, Jesus made it very clear that the kingdom he was proclaiming was *not* a national, political structure. Rather He proclaimed that His *kingdom was not of this world*. The major theme of Jesus' teaching was that he had come to establish a kingdom that brought spiritual life to individuals and social justice into society.

> Pilate then went back inside the palace, summoned Jesus and asked him, "Are you the king of the Jews?" Is that your own idea, Jesus asked, or did others talk to you about me? "Am I a Jew?" Pilate replied. "Your own people and chief priests handed you over to me. What is it you have done?" Jesus said, "*My kingdom is not of this world*. If it were, my servants would fight to prevent my arrest by the Jewish leaders. But now my kingdom is from another place." "You are a king, then!" said Pilate. Jesus answered, "You say that I am a king." (John 18:33–37[1])
>
> Now this is *eternal life: that they know you,* the only true God, and Jesus Christ, whom you have sent. (John 17:3[1])

> The Spirit of the Lord is on me, because he has anointed me to proclaim good news to the *poor*. He has sent me to proclaim freedom for the *prisoners* and recovery of sight for the *blind*, to set the *oppressed* free, to proclaim the year of the Lord's favor. (Luke 4:18–19^E)

In the first year of Jesus' public teaching and healing, he encountered opposition and criticism, particularly from legalistic Jewish leaders called the Pharisees (Mark 2:13–3:7^E). Jesus' response to the Pharisees' criticisms provided profound insight into the nature of the kingdom that he intended to establish on earth. When the Pharisees asked why Jesus ate with "sinners and tax collectors" (Mark 2:16^E), he answered them,

> It is not the healthy who need a doctor, but the sick. I have not come to call the righteous, but sinners. (Mark 2:17^E)

The Pharisees asked him why his disciples did not fast. Jesus answered,

> How can the guests of the bridegroom fast while he is with them? They cannot, so long as they have him with them. (Mark 2:19^E)
>
> No one sews a patch of unshrunk cloth on an old garment. Otherwise, the new piece will pull away from the old, making the tear worse. And no one pours new wine into old wineskins. Otherwise, the wine will burst the skins, and both the wine and the wineskins will be ruined. No, they pour new wine into new wineskins. (Mark 2:21–22^E)

The Pharisees asked him why his disciples picked some grain to eat on the Sabbath, which was against their traditions. Jesus answered,

> The Sabbath was made for man, not man for the Sabbath. So the Son of Man is Lord even of the Sabbath. (Mark 2:27–28^E)

These responses by Jesus describe the nature of his kingdom. The mission of the kingdom will be spiritual healing of individuals. The characteristic of kingdom members will be joy because Jesus has come to offer relationship with God. Many of the old Jewish structures and practices will be abandoned, religious rules will take second place to human need. The kingdom of God was, and is, a spiritual affiliation of those who *follow* and *believe* Jesus and thus gain a relationship with God and other believers. His kingdom is evidenced as Jesus' followers reflect the loving and just character of God into society.

The Foundations of God's Kingdom—Jesus' Sacrificial Death and Resurrection

Jesus' petition "Our Father ... your kingdom come" was in part a prayer that the Father would give him the strength to fulfill his mission of sacrificial death. At the outset of Jesus' ministry, the prophet John the Baptist proclaimed that Jesus' life would involve sacrifice.

> The next day John saw Jesus coming toward him and said, "Look, *the Lamb of God, who takes away the sin of the world!*" (John 1:29^D)

John was referring to the sacrificial lambs that were offered in the temple as atonement for the sins of the people. John was prophetically foreshadowing the sacrificial death that Jesus would suffer as atonement for human sin.

Jesus frequently taught the disciples that he must die in order to establish his kingdom.

> He then began to teach them that the Son of Man must suffer many things and be rejected by the elders, the chief priests and the teachers of the law, and that *he must be killed* and after three days rise again. (Mark 8:31^G)
>
> Now Jesus was going up to Jerusalem. On the way, he took the Twelve aside and said to them, "We are going up to Jerusalem, and the Son of Man will be delivered over to the chief priests and the teachers of the law. *They will condemn him to death and will hand him over to the Gentiles to be mocked and flogged and crucified.* On the third day he will be raised to life!" (Matt. 20:17–19^H)

On the night before his crucifixion, Jesus prayed in great agony for the strength to complete his destiny.

> Jesus went out as usual to the Mount of Olives, and his disciples followed him. . . . He withdrew about a stone's throw beyond them, knelt down and prayed, Father, if you are willing, take this cup from me; *yet not my will, but yours be done.* An angel from heaven appeared to him and strengthened him. And being in anguish, he prayed more earnestly, and his sweat was like drops of blood falling to the ground. (Luke 22:39–43^J)

Jesus taught that his death for the forgiveness of sins was at the heart of the Christian story. Before he was crucified, Jesus instituted what has been termed "the Eucharist" (meaning "thanksgiving") as a memorial of his death, clearly establishing the centrality of his crucifixion. The cross has become the foremost Christian symbol.

> While they were eating, Jesus took bread, and when he had given thanks, he broke it and gave it to his disciples, saying, "Take and eat; this is my body." Then he took a cup, and when he had given thanks, he gave it to them, saying, "Drink from it, all of you. *This is my blood of the covenant, which is poured out for many for the forgiveness of sins.* I tell you; I will not drink from this fruit of the vine from now on until that day when I drink it new with you in my Father's kingdom." (Matt 26:26–29[1])

In the providence of God, the death and resurrection of Jesus are the essential foundation of God's kingdom and the basis of an intimate relationship with God. This reality was well understood by the early Christians. The apostle Paul's testimony was the following:

> I have been crucified with Christ and I no longer live, but *Christ lives in me.* The life I now live in the body, I live by faith in the Son of God, who *loved me and gave himself for me.* (Gal. 2:20)

The substitutionary death of Christ allows us entry into a Christ-mediated fellowship with God or, as Jesus called it, *eternal life.* God's kingdom is composed of those who receive and reflect the *forgiveness* of God.

Even as Jesus focused attention on his earthly death as the way in which he chose to be remembered, he indicated to his disciples that his death would not be the end of his existence. He stated,

> I will not drink from this fruit of the vine from now on *until that day when I drink it new with you in my Father's kingdom.* (Matt. 26:29[I])

Jesus coupled the prediction of his death with the assurance that he would return to life in power. He said to his disciples,

> The Son of Man is going to be delivered into the hands of men. They will kill him, and *after three days he will rise.* (Mark 9:31[H])

Jesus proclaimed that the duality of his death and resurrection was the gateway to the new type of relationship with God and the means of bringing God's kingdom into the world, and establishing the eternal nature of the kingdom.

After his resurrection, Jesus made direct reference to those who would continue the growth of his kingdom after he had left the earth. He said to his disciple, Thomas,

> Because you have seen me, you have believed; blessed are those *who have not seen and yet have believed.* (John 20:29[L])

Jesus' final words to his followers were about the spread of his kingdom after his departure from the world.

All authority in heaven and *on earth has been given to me*. Therefore, *go and make disciples of all nations*, baptizing them in the name of the Father and of the Son and of the Holy Spirit, and teaching them to obey everything I have commanded you. And surely I am with you always, to the very end of the age. (Matt. 28:18–20^L)

This teaching is known as the Great Commission. Jesus begins it with the astounding claim *"All authority in heaven and earth* has been given to me." Such a statement is only possible in the context of God's power as demonstrated by Jesus' resurrection. The experience of the risen Jesus inspired the early Christian community to witness boldly against the powers of the age. The apostle Paul proclaimed this faith,

Therefore, God exalted him to the highest place and gave him the name that is above every name, that at the name of Jesus every knee should bow, in heaven and on earth and under the earth, and every tongue acknowledge that *Jesus Christ is Lord*, to the glory of God the Father. (Phil. 2:9–11)

Jesus' death, resurrection and exaltation are the foundation of God's kingdom.

The Empowerment of God's Kingdom – The Presence of the Spirit of God

Jesus taught that after his death and resurrection, his presence would continue in the world through the arrival of God's Spirit. Jesus told his disciples,

> And I will ask the Father, and he will give you another advocate to help you and be with you forever—the *Spirit of truth*. The world cannot accept him, because it neither sees him nor knows him. But you know him, for he lives with you and will be in you. (John 14:16–17[1])

About twenty-five years after Jesus left the earth, the apostle Paul explained how the historical fact of Jesus' death and resurrection was translated into a living reality through the action of God's Spirit.

> But when the set time had fully come, God sent his Son, born of a woman, born under the law, to redeem those under the law, that we might receive adoption to sonship. Because you are his sons, *God sent the Spirit of his Son into our hearts, the Spirit who calls out, "Abba, Father."* (Gal. 4:4–6)

The kingdom of God and of his Son could not be fulfilled without the presence of God's Spirit in the world. The apostle Paul's words make it very clear that after Jesus was no longer physically present, a personal relationship with the Father could occur through the action of God's Spirit.

Early in Jesus public ministry, he taught about the essential role of God's Spirit in the coming of God's kingdom. A Jewish leader, Nicodemus, came to question Jesus about his teachings. He answered,

> Very truly I tell you, no one can enter the *kingdom of God* unless they are born of water and *the Spirit*. Flesh gives birth to flesh, *but the Spirit gives birth to spirit.* You

should not be surprised at my saying, "*You must be born again*." The wind blows wherever it pleases. You hear its sound, but you cannot tell where it comes from or where it is going. So it is with everyone *born of the Spirit*. (John 3:5–8[D])

In our time, the term "born again" is often used to identify a particular type of Christian. However, Jesus taught that all his followers would be "born again," receiving a new life and identity through the Spirit of God and becoming birthright citizens of God's kingdom.

Toward the end of his life, Jesus instructed the disciples about the role of God's Spirit in the ongoing progress of his kingdom:

> But very truly I tell you, it is for your good that I am going away. Unless I go away, *the Advocate will not come to you; but if I go, I will send him to you.* When he comes, he will prove the world to be in the wrong about sin and righteousness and judgment. . . . When he, *the Spirit of truth*, comes, he *will guide you into all the truth*. He will not speak on his own; he will speak only what he hears and he will tell you what is yet to come. He will glorify me because it is *from me that he will receive what he will make known to you.* (John 16:7–14[I])

Jesus' prophecy, that God's Spirit would continue to unfold God's truth after his death and resurrection, was demonstrated in the miraculous growth of the early Christian community. In the longer perspective of the Christian story, the *Spirit-inspired* writings, the New Testament Gospels and Epistles, have been the essential source for communicating Jesus' living message to the world.

The Members of God's Kingdom—Believers in Jesus as the Son of God

As quoted above, Jesus stated that entry into God's kingdom is enabled by God's Spirit (John 3:5^D). However, Jesus and his early followers also taught that the privileges of membership in God's kingdom, salvation, and eternal life were granted through *personal belief that Jesus is the Son of God*. This message is "the gospel."

> God so loved the world that he gave his only Son, that whoever *believes* in him shall not perish but have eternal life. (John 3:16^D)

Jesus' last recorded words proclaimed the saving power of believing the gospel.

> Go into all the world and proclaim the gospel to all creation. Whoever *believes and is baptized will be saved*, but whoever does not believe will be condemned. (Mark 16:15–16^L)

Jesus claimed that as the Son of God, he was the ultimate source of life and the "way" to relationship with God (John 14:6), and that *belief in him* was the source of spiritual food and drink and, ultimately, eternal life.

> I am the bread of life. Whoever comes to me will never go hungry, and whoever *believes in me* will never be thirsty. . . . For my Father's will is that everyone who looks to the Son and *believes in him* shall have eternal life, and I will raise them up at the last day. (John 6:35, 40^G)

I am the resurrection and the life. The one who *believes in me* will live, even though they die, and whoever lives by believing in me will never die. *Do you believe this?* (John 11:25–26^H)

Thus, in the purposes of God and enabled by the Spirit of God, everyone who looks to the Son and believes in him becomes a family member in God's eternal kingdom.

After his resurrection and before he physically departed from the earth, Jesus made a very important statement about belief in him. Thomas, one of the disciples who had not yet witnessed Jesus' person after his resurrection, refused to believe until he saw Jesus and touched his wounds. When Jesus did appear, Thomas exclaimed, "My Lord and My God!"

> Then Jesus told him, "Because you have seen me, you have believed; *blessed are those who have not seen and yet have believed.*" (John 20:28–29^L)

Many years after Jesus' death and resurrection, when the Christian community had expanded throughout the Roman Empire, John the disciple wrote,

> To all who *did receive him, to those who believed in his name*, he gave the right to become children of God. (John 1:12^D)

> These [things] are written that *you may believe that Jesus is the Messiah, the Son of God, and that by believing you may have life in his name.* (John 20:31^L)

In the writings of the apostles, belief in Jesus was most often referred to as "faith in Christ." The apostle Paul wrote to the Christian community at Philippi, describing himself as,

> not having a righteousness of my own from the law but that which is through faith in Christ—*the righteousness that comes from God on the basis of faith.* (Phil. 3:9)

In the Christian story, belief in Jesus imparts righteousness and spiritual life from God and is the ground upon which a Christian life of gratitude and service may be built.

From the beginning, and through the centuries it has become evident that "belief in Jesus" is not formulaic but is progressive and differs with individuals. Luke's record in the Acts of the Apostles demonstrates that some were believers because they had witnessed Jesus' life, death, and resurrection, and others, such as the apostle Paul, became believers through miraculous intervention. However, most became believers through the witness of other Christ followers. Belief was often, but not always, accompanied by baptism as a personal and public witness.

Many have believed in the context of a Christian culture; others have believed against the grain of their society and have suffered much for their belief. Christian belief will be evidenced by personal and lifestyle characteristics that reflect the principles of Jesus' teaching. However, these behaviors are demonstrated in a wide variety of ways in different cultures and perceptions and therefore relate to the circumstances of time and place.

In the reality of daily living, Christians associate with others who are "believers" in Jesus for fellowship and service. However, as Jesus clearly taught in parables to be discussed below, God is the ultimate judge of those who are members of the kingdom.

The People and Growth of God's Kingdom

The Christian story began with a diverse group of men and women. Jesus' twelve apostles included: Peter, Andrew, James, and John, and some other fishermen from Galilee; but also, Matthew, a tax collector and Roman collaborator, Simon the Zealot, probably an anti-Roman activist and, Judas, his betrayer (Luke 6:12-16[F]).

Women were much involved in the early Christian story. Foremost was Jesus' mother, Mary, who followed him until his crucifixion. Around the time of Jesus' birth, Mary prophesied,

> My soul glorifies the Lord
> and my spirit rejoices in God my Savior,
> for he has been mindful
> of the humble state of his servant.
> From now on all generations will call me blessed,
> for the Mighty One has done great things for me—
> holy is his name. . . (Luke 1:46-49[A])

Jesus' mother was the initiator of his first miracle when he turned the water into wine at a wedding in Cana of Galilee.

> When the wine ran out, the mother of Jesus said to him, "They have no wine." And Jesus said to her, "Woman, what does this have to do with me? My hour has not yet come." His mother said to the servants, "Do whatever he tells you." (John 2:1-12^D)

While Jesus was on the cross, he appointed his disciple John to care for his mother,

> Near the cross of Jesus stood his mother, his mother's sister, Mary the wife of Clopas, and Mary Magdalene. When Jesus saw his mother there, and the disciple whom he loved standing nearby, he said to her, "Woman, here is your son," and to the disciple, "Here is your mother." From that time on, this disciple took her into his home. (John 19:25-27^K)

Jesus had a surprisingly significant conversation about the true nature of worship, with a Samaritan woman whom he met while walking from Jerusalem to Galilee. Given the cultural norms of the time and animosity between Jews and Samaritans, it is truly remarkable that this conversation took place and, it demonstrated Jesus' disdain for cultural barriers.

> "Woman, Jesus replied, believe me, a time is coming when you will worship the Father neither on this mountain nor in Jerusalem... Yet a time is coming and has now come when the true worshipers will worship the Father in the Spirit and in truth, for they are the kind of worshipers the Father seeks. *God is spirit, and his worshipers must worship in the Spirit and in truth."* The woman said, "I know that Messiah" (called Christ) "is

coming. When he comes, he will explain everything to us." Then Jesus declared, "I, the one speaking to you—I am he." (John 4:21-26[D])

Martha and Mary were sisters in the town of Bethany who opened their home to Jesus when he was in the Jerusalem area. (Luke 10:38[H]) Jesus developed a very close relationship with them, John noted, "Jesus loved Martha and her sister and her brother Lazarus." (John 11:16[H]) At the time of Lazarus death, Jesus and the disciples came to their home in Bethany. Before he raised Lazarus, Jesus had a profound discussion with Martha, Jesus said,

> "Your brother will rise again." "Martha answered, "I know he will rise again in the resurrection at the last day." Jesus said to her, "I am the resurrection and the life. The one who believes in me will live, even though they die; and whoever lives by believing in me will never die. Do you believe this?" "Yes, Lord," she replied, "I believe that you are the Messiah, the Son of God, who is to come into the world." (John 11:23-27[1])

After Jesus' own resurrection, the women disciples were the first to discover that he had risen and, Mary Magdalene was the first person to see the risen Jesus.

> Early on the first day of the week, while it was still dark, Mary Magdalene went to the tomb and saw that the stone had been removed from the entrance. So she came running to Simon Peter and the other disciple, the one Jesus loved, and said, "They have taken the Lord out of the tomb, and we don't know where they have put him!" (John 20:1-2[L])

Peter and John ran to the tomb and not finding Jesus, they went back to where they were staying.

> Now Mary stood outside the tomb crying. As she wept, she bent over to look into the tomb and saw two angels in white, seated where Jesus' body had been, one at the head and the other at the foot. They asked her, "Woman, why are you crying?" "They have taken my Lord away," she said, "and I don't know where they have put him." At this, she turned around and saw Jesus standing there, but she did not realize that it was Jesus. He asked her, "Woman, why are you crying? Who is it you are looking for?" Thinking he was the gardener, she said, "Sir, if you have carried him away, tell me where you have put him, and I will get him." Jesus said to her, "Mary." She turned toward him and cried out in Aramaic, "Rabboni!" (which means teacher) (John 20:11-16^L)

For the next forty days Jesus appeared to various groups of disciples until he was finally taken from them (Acts 1:4-9^L).

From the beginning, an important aspect of the Christian story has been about reaching out and spreading the good news of Jesus' kingdom. When he called his first disciples from their fishing, Jesus said to them,

> Come, follow me," . . . and I will send you out to fish for people. (Matt. 4:1^E)

As his followers grew in number, Jesus continued to send them out.

> After this the Lord appointed seventy-two others and sent them two by two ahead of him to every town and place where he was about to go. He told them, "The harvest is plentiful, but the workers are few. Ask the Lord of the harvest, therefore, to send out workers into his harvest field." (Luke 10: 1,2^H)

Jesus last recorded words were a commission to his followers to take his teaching to all people.

> Therefore, go and make disciples of all nations, baptizing them in the name of the Father and of the Son and of the Holy Spirit, and teaching them to obey everything I have commanded you. (Matt. 28:19-20^L)

Before Jesus ascended from the earth, he predicted the future growth of his kingdom.

> But you will receive power when the Holy Spirit comes on you; and you will be my witnesses in Jerusalem, and in all Judea and Samaria, *and to the ends of the earth."* (Acts 1:8^L)

Ten days later, Luke described the dramatic coming of the Holy Spirit upon the followers of Jesus. (Acts 2:1-13^L) This experience initiated the rapid expansion of the early Christian community to thousands of men and women.

In the early years after Jesus' death and resurrection, the Christian community grew in Jerusalem and into the surrounding area. Some of this initial spread was given impetus by persecution. Gentiles began to join the community and after about ten years, the Christians in the city of Antioch undertook an intentional mission to spread the news of God's kingdom to other regions. They sent out the apostle Paul and Barnabas to witness in Jewish synagogues west and north of Antioch. Subsequently, Paul and others undertook further missionary journeys, *with increasing focus on non-Jewish converts, reaching as far as Rome.*

The fledgling churches in Europe became established. The letters to these churches from Paul and other apostles, and the written Gospels, became foundational documents for the worldwide Christian church. Thus, the Christian gospel spread from its Jewish base into the diverse Greco-Roman world, through North Africa, Europe, and beyond. Today, "Christianity" is the largest religion in the world, comprising over two billion followers.

Communal Life in God's Kingdom—The Church

Jesus taught that *loving relationships* between his followers is to be the most significant symbol of his kingdom.

> By this everyone will know that you are my disciples, if you love one another. (John 13:35[1])

Christian kingdom living has been characterized by communities that worship, learn, pray, and serve together. As will be discussed later, Jesus had much to say about the Christian community and how love was to be manifest there and in society.

Communal worship was very much a part of Jesus' life and, therefore, kingdom living. Jesus was first introduced in the Gospel of Luke when he was twelve years old, in the temple, "sitting among the teachers, listening to them and asking them questions" (Luke 2:46^B). Jesus' next public appearance was on the Sabbath, in the synagogue "as was his custom;" there he opened the scroll and taught (Luke 4:16-23^E). Jesus' frequent attendance at the synagogues and the temple is a clear model of regular communal worship, which became a significant feature of the Christian church.

Community participation in *the Lord's Supper*, the "Eucharist," or "Communion," is an important aspect of Christian community life. This ritual was established by Jesus on the evening before he died, at the time of Jewish Passover.

> When the hour came, Jesus and his apostles reclined at the table. And he said to them, "I have eagerly desired to eat this Passover with you before I suffer. For I tell you, I will not eat it again until it finds fulfillment in the kingdom of God." After taking the cup, he gave thanks and said, "Take this and divide it among you. For I tell you I will not drink again from the fruit of the vine until the kingdom of God comes." And he took bread, gave thanks and broke it, and gave it to them, saying, "This is my body given for you; do this in remembrance of me." In the same way, after the supper he took the cup, saying, "This cup is the *new covenant in my blood*, which is poured out for you." (Luke 22:14-20^I)

Jesus introduced a memorial ritual that would look back, not on his profound teaching or miracles, but on his death, the counterintuitive symbol of his kingdom. Jesus replaced the Jewish Passover meal, which recalled God's deliverance of Israel from captivity in Egypt, with a *new symbolism for his worldwide kingdom.* The Jewish Passover celebration denoted a covenant between God and the Hebrew nation based on obedience to "the law" written in the Old Testament. Jesus' *new covenant* was established by his death and resurrection and was to be memorialized by communal breaking of bread and drinking of wine.

The new covenant, based on *God's forgiveness*, is open to all humankind and is entered into by believing in his Son, Jesus Christ. As recorded in the book of Acts, the Eucharist has been practiced since the earliest days of the Christian community, usually on "the first day of the week" (Acts 20:7). This foundational symbolic act of Jesus' kingdom continues to be regularly celebrated in a wide diversity of forms throughout the world.

Christian baptism is the other important symbol of Jesus' kingdom. Jesus taught about baptism in the last words he spoke before he left the earth:

> Therefore go and make disciples of all nations, *baptizing them in the name of the Father and of the Son and of the Holy Spirit*, and teaching them to obey everything I have commanded you. And surely I am with you always, to the very end of the age. (Matt. 28:19–20[L])

Again, Jesus completely changed the symbolism of baptism, from the Jewish ritual of cleansing to a Christian ritual that signifies cleansing and new life in the power of the trinitarian "name of the Father, Son and Holy Spirit." Jesus himself was baptized in the Jewish context by John the Baptist. Luke tells us,

> When all the people were being baptized, Jesus was baptized too. And as he was praying, heaven was opened and the Holy Spirit descended on him in bodily form like a dove. And a voice came from heaven: "You are my Son, whom I love; with you I am well pleased." (Luke 3:21–23^C)

The book of Acts records that the new baptism was practiced from the earliest days of the Christian community. The apostle Paul explained its meaning.

> Don't you know that all of us who were baptized into Christ Jesus were baptized into his death? We were therefore buried with him through baptism into death in order that, just as Christ was raised from the dead through the glory of the Father, we too may *live a new life*. (Rom. 6:3–4)

About thirty years after Jesus's ascension, his disciple Peter wrote a profound description of *the church* in a letter to Christian communities in Asia (1 Peter 2:4–12). He described the church as a spiritual building, secured by Christ as the cornerstone, a priesthood of believers called upon to declare the praises of God and to live sacrificial lives for the good of humankind.

The Fulfillment of God's Kingdom—Eternal Life and Justice

As previously noted, when Jesus instituted the Eucharistic memorial, he referenced yet a further coming of the kingdom beyond this earth. Though the kingdom of God began to exist on earth with the coming of Jesus, it extends beyond his earthly life. Luke described Jesus' teaching about the future kingdom at the last supper he had with his disciples.

> When the hour came, Jesus and his apostles reclined at the table. And he said to them, "I have eagerly desired to eat this Passover with you before I suffer. For I tell you, I will not eat it again until it *finds fulfillment in the kingdom of God.*" After taking the cup, he gave thanks and said, "Take this and divide it among you. For I tell you I will not drink again from the fruit of the vine until the *kingdom of God comes.*" (Luke 22:14–18[1])

Thus, when we pray "your kingdom come," we pray also for the final fulfillment in the kingdom of God about which Jesus taught:

> When the Son of Man comes in his glory, and all the angels with him, he will sit on his glorious throne. All the nations will be gathered before him, and he will separate the people one from another as a shepherd separates the sheep from the goats. He will put the sheep on his right and the goats on his left.
>
> Then the King will say to those on his right, "Come, you who are blessed by my Father; take your inheritance, *the kingdom prepared for you since the creation*

of the world. For I was hungry and you gave me something to eat, I was thirsty and you gave me something to drink, I was a stranger and you invited me in, I needed clothes and you clothed me, I was sick and you looked after me, I was in prison and you came to visit me. . . . Truly I tell you, whatever you did for one of the least of these brothers and sisters of mine, you did for me."

Then he will say to those on his left, "Depart from me, you who are cursed, into the eternal fire prepared for the devil and his angels. For I was hungry and you gave me nothing to eat, I was thirsty and you gave me nothing to drink, I was a stranger and you did not invite me in, I needed clothes and you did not clothe me, I was sick and in prison and you did not look after me. . . . Truly I tell you, whatever you did not do for one of the least of these, you did not do for me." Then they will go away to eternal punishment, but the righteous to eternal life. (Matt. 25:31–46[I])

These words of Jesus are a vivid reminder of what he said when he first claimed to be the Messiah. He came to bless the poor, heal the sick, and free the imprisoned (Luke 4:18[E]). Jesus expected that his kingdom followers would generously provide for the physical and social needs of others. He strongly condemned those who neglected such charity.

Thus, Jesus' teaching about the ultimate coming of his kingdom had two aspects. First, as signified by the last words *but the righteous to eternal life*, it means eternal relationship with God. This is the joyous hope of the Christian story. However, the second aspect of the future kingdom is judgment and final justice. It is relevant that an aspect of the final judgment is based on obedience to the second great commandment, *love your neighbor as yourself*. The teaching of Jesus proclaimed judgment on sins of omission, what was not done for others, as well as sins of commission, what was done to harm others.

In summary, the phrase, *your kingdom come*, encompasses the grand scope of the Christian story from the advent of Jesus Christ, God's Son on earth, to his eternal kingdom beyond time. Jesus' kingdom began with his teaching and healing ministry and continued to grow as a community of Jesus' followers experienced life with him. Jesus' death and resurrection provided the way to relationship with God for all in the future who would believe. God's Holy Spirit is the power that has brought the kingdom into the lives of individuals and into society over the past two thousand years. The kingdom is advanced by "the church," a community of believers who teach, pray, worship, and serve. Loving service and participation in baptism and the Eucharist identify membership in the kingdom. Jesus promised a final fulfillment of his kingdom that will include eternal life beyond this earthly existence and the fulfillment of ultimate justice.

Jesus' Parables Illustrate Important Truths About God's Kingdom.

Jesus taught using a series of parables to explain the nature of his kingdom. First, Jesus claimed that those who find their way into his kingdom have come upon the greatest possible treasure in life. However, it should be noted that Jesus' teaching implied that considerable cost was involved.

> The kingdom of heaven is like treasure hidden in a field. When a man found it, he hid it again, and then in his joy went and sold all he had and bought that field. Again, the kingdom of heaven is like a merchant looking for fine pearls. When he found one of great value, he went away and sold everything he had and bought it. (Matt. 13:44–46^F)

Second, Jesus taught that entry into his kingdom would be accomplished by hearing and receiving his teaching. Further, he taught that only some of those who heard his word would enter the kingdom. Jesus compared his kingdom teaching to a farmer sowing seed. Much of the seed fell on infertile areas such as on stones, hardened pathways, or weeds. However, some seed fell on *good soil* and produced fruit. Jesus explained the meaning of the parable.

> But the seed falling on good soil refers to someone who hears *the word and understands it*. (Matt. 13:23^F)

An illustration of this parable is recorded in Mark's Gospel.

> As Jesus started on his way, a man ran up to him and fell on his knees before him. "Good teacher," he asked, "what must I do to inherit eternal life?" "Why do you call me good?" Jesus answered. "No one is good—except God alone. You know the commandments: 'You shall not murder, you shall not commit adultery, you shall not steal, you shall not give false testimony, you shall not defraud, honor your father and mother.'" "Teacher," he declared, "all these I have kept since I was

a boy." Jesus looked at him and loved him. "One thing you lack," he said. "Go, sell everything you have and give to the poor, and you will have treasure in heaven. Then come, follow me." At this the man's face fell. He went away sad, because he had great wealth. Jesus looked around and said to his disciples, "How hard it is for the rich to enter the kingdom of God!" (Mark 10:17–33[H])

Jesus taught that not everyone who initially responds to him will enter the kingdom. The cost of following Jesus may seem too high for many.

On one occasion when Jesus was talking with his disciples, he made the demands and rewards of kingdom membership very clear to them.

> Whoever wants to be my disciple must deny themselves and take up their cross daily and follow me. For whoever wants to save their life will lose it, but whoever loses their life for me will save it. What good is it for someone to gain the whole world, and yet lose or forfeit their very self? (Luke 9:23–25[G])

Third, Jesus stated that his kingdom would flourish, intermixed in an imperfect society from which it could not be separated until the coming of the final kingdom. Jesus again compared the kingdom to a farmer who planted good seed in his field. While he was sleeping, an enemy planted weeds, and the wheat and the weeds grew up together. The servants asked the farmer whether they should pull up the weeds. His answer was,

> No...because while you are pulling the weeds you may uproot the wheat with them. Let both grow together

> until the harvest. At that time I will tell the harvesters: First collect the weeds and tie them in bundles to be burned; then gather the wheat and bring it into my barn. (Matt. 13:29–30^F)

Fourth, Jesus claimed that his kingdom, though seemingly insignificant at the beginning, would grow dramatically and would permeate society.

> The kingdom of heaven is like a mustard seed. . . . Though it is the smallest of all seeds, yet when it grows, it is the largest of garden plants and becomes a tree. . . . The kingdom of heaven is like yeast that a woman took and mixed into about sixty pounds of flour until it worked all through the dough. (Matt. 13:31–33^F)

Fifth, Jesus taught that not everyone who was associated with the kingdom would, in fact, be a kingdom member. Just as in the parable of the wheat and the tares, it is important to recognize that, ultimately, God is the judge concerning those who are members of his kingdom.

Jesus described his kingdom as a net that was let down into a lake and caught many fish.

> Then they sat down and collected the good fish in baskets, but threw the bad away. This is how it will be at the end of the age. The angels will come and separate the wicked from the righteous. (Matt. 13:48–49^F)

This somewhat strange parable is important since, throughout history, many associated with the Christian community have done much wickedness. This parable clearly portrays that association with God's kingdom does not preclude being judged for wicked actions.

To summarize, in these parables, Jesus explained the expectations for his kingdom: Finding the reality of the kingdom is costly but is a value worth full commitment. Many who hear God's word do not enter the kingdom. Though the kingdom had small roots and at times seems fragile, in fact, it has and continues to have an immense impact on society. The umbrella of the apparent kingdom contains good and bad members; however, the completion of the kingdom will not be realized until God's final judgment.

5

The Third Petition: "Your Will Be Done on Earth as It Is in Heaven"

Justo Gonzales summarizes the writings of early church leaders as follows: "The ancient Christian writers seem to be in general agreement that this petition regarding the will of God is above all a plea that God will help us to obey the divine will, as well as a commitment to do so."[11] With the phrase "your will be *done on earth* as it is in heaven," Jesus taught that even though God's moral will is universal, Jesus' concern was very much about the moral actions of his followers in the daily discourse of life on earth. This emphasis is strongly reinforced in the later writings of his disciples.

The Christian story begins with the premise that human beings have been given the capacity to make moral choices, to exercise their own will. The earliest narrative in the Bible, the book of Genesis, is a story of human resistance to the will of God. The subsequent biblical record is one of constant defiance of God's moral directives. In his important book *The Political Meaning of Christianity*, Glenn Tinder writes that the highest God-given human capacity is free will, "a freedom real enough to enable [humans] to defy God and oppose his will."[12] The Hebrews were given God's commandments by Moses, but even the best of them failed to fully adhere to the Ten Commandments (see appendix 3).

Jesus was in frequent conflict with the religious leaders of his day, whom he accused of failing to fulfill the greater purposes of God's will. On one occasion Jesus condemned their hypocrisy saying,

> Woe to you, teachers of the law and Pharisees, you hypocrites! You give a tenth of your spices—mint, dill, and cumin. But you have neglected the *more important matters of the law—justice, mercy and faithfulness.* You should have practiced the latter, without neglecting the former. (Matt. 23:23[1])

Jesus grieved in exasperation as he observed the human will being opposed to God's will.

> Jerusalem, Jerusalem, you who kill the prophets and stone those sent to you, how often I have longed to gather your children together, as a hen gathers her chicks under her wings, and *you were not willing.* (Matt. 23:37[1])

Jesus' most succinct definition of God's will on earth arose during an interaction between him and religious leaders. Jesus was asked which is the greatest commandment. He answered by quoting from the Mosaic law:

> Hear, O Israel: The Lord our God, the Lord is one. Love the Lord your God with all your heart and with all your soul and with all your mind and with all your

strength. The second is this: Love your neighbor as yourself. There is no commandment greater than these. (Mark 12:29–31[1])

It is important to understand these commandments from a Christian perspective. It is the will of God for human beings to love him and love their neighbors, but the standard is extremely high—to love God with all your emotion, will, and intellect, to give your neighbor the same care as yourself. It is well demonstrated throughout biblical and human history that such a level of love for God and neighbor has never been achieved except in the person of Jesus.

The core message of Jesus was that even though human beings are unable to achieve God's moral standards, they will be *forgiven* if they recognize their need and accept the "good news" provided by Jesus' life, death, and resurrection. The necessity of repentance was the first teaching of Jesus immediately after he was baptized:

> The kingdom of God has come near. "Repent and believe the good news!" (Mark 1:15[C]).

Christian living is aspirational, enabled by the realization that *Jesus' followers live forgiven lives*. Jesus made the importance of *human repentance and God's forgiveness* very clear in some of his last words to his disciples before leaving the earth.

> The Messiah will suffer and rise from the dead on the third day, and *repentance for the forgiveness of sins* will be preached in his name to all nations. (Luke 24:46–47[L])

The first step in fulfilling the will of God is the personal acknowledgement of sin and repentance.

What is God's Will? — Loving God and Loving Neighbor

In his book *Christian Counter-Culture*, John R. W. Stott writes,

> We are constantly under pressure to conform to the self-centeredness of secular culture.... But in the Christian counter-culture our top concern is not our name, kingdom and will but God's. Whether we can pray these petitions with integrity is a searching test of the reality and depth of our Christian profession.[13]

Christians seek to do God's will, to love God and neighbor, in response to God's love as demonstrated through Jesus Christ. Much of Jesus' teaching was about how his followers were to live out the will of God in everyday life. These teachings are not to be seen as laws but as instruction and tutoring. In this context, it is important to understand that Christians live under the cover of God's forgiveness. It is not possible for us to live fully righteous lives, but our desire to do God's will is motivated by God's mercy. Living the will of God is an ongoing process of learning in the context of Christian community, enabled by God's Spirit.

It is important to note the example of Jesus who was totally committed to doing the will of the Father.

> "My food," said Jesus, "is *to do the will of him who sent me* and to finish his work." (John 4:34[D])

> My Father, if it is possible, let this cup pass from me. Yet not as I will, *but as you will*. (Matt. 26:39[I])

Jesus illustrated the commandment to *love your neighbor as yourself* with the well-known parable of the good Samaritan which he told to an expert in the law.

A Jewish man, walking from Jerusalem to Jericho, was robbed, beaten, and left by the side of the road. His plight was ignored by a passing priest and a Levite, but a Samaritan, despised by the Jews because of religious differences, "took pity on him."

> He went to him and bandaged his wounds, pouring on oil and wine. Then he put the man on his own donkey, brought him to an inn and took care of him. . . . "Look after him," he said, "and when I return, I will reimburse you for any extra expense you may have."
>
> [Jesus asked,] "Which of these three do you think was a neighbor to the man who fell into the hands of robbers?" The expert in the law replied, "The one who had mercy on him."
>
> Jesus told him, "Go and do likewise." (Luke 10:33–37[H])

According to Jesus, it is the will of God that his followers provide care for those in need, those whom we pass on the path of life, without regard to race or religion. The remarkable growth of the early Christian communities is attributed to the care they gave to the sick and needy and to the inclusion of people from all backgrounds and nationalities.[14]

It is Jesus' will that we love all human beings, but as previously noted, it is his will that his followers specifically love one another. When he was teaching his disciples shortly before his death, he modeled for them the type of life they were to lead. He took the place of a servant and washed their feet. Then he said to them,

> A new command I give you: Love one another. As I have loved you, so you must love one another. By this everyone will know that you are my disciples, if you love one another. (John 13:34–35[I])

After God's great command to "love your neighbor as yourself" is Jesus' "new command" for his followers to "love one another." This "new command" is critical to the growth of Jesus' kingdom; thus, all his teachings about living God's will must be applied particularly to the life of the Christian community.

Doing God's Will—Jesus' Teaching in the Sermon on the Mount

Jesus' most comprehensive teaching about living God's will has been compiled into the Sermon on the Mount, recorded in Matthew 5–7[E]. The first part of this teaching, designated as the Beatitudes, is a summary of attitudes and behaviors that are to characterize citizens in Jesus' kingdom. These are not entry qualifications for God's kingdom but a description of mindsets and actions that should distinguish followers of Jesus as they are empowered by God's Spirit. Jesus taught,

> Blessed are the *poor in spirit*,
>   for theirs is the kingdom of heaven.
> Blessed are those who *mourn*,
>   for they will be comforted.

Blessed are the *meek*,
   for they will inherit the earth.
Blessed are those who *hunger and thirst for righteousness*,
   for they will be filled.
Blessed are the *merciful*,
   for they will be shown mercy.
Blessed are the *pure in heart*,
   for they will see God.
Blessed are the *peacemakers*,
   for they will be called children of God.
Blessed are those who are *persecuted because of righteousness*,
   for theirs is the kingdom of heaven. (Matt. 5:1–12^E)

Many books have been written about the depth of meaning in these poetic words. However, when Jesus gave this discourse to his disciples, there was a plain meaning that was consistent with all his teaching. Those who are members of his kingdom are blessed by God and will be characterized by the moral values and actions that Jesus described. These statements will be considered more fully.

"Blessed are the poor in spirit"—Those who recognize their spiritual need

Jesus' first teaching proclaimed that *his mission was to bring good news to those in need*.

> The Spirit of the Lord is on me, because he has anointed me to proclaim *good news to the poor*. He has sent me to proclaim freedom for the prisoners and recovery

of sight for the blind, to set the oppressed free. (Luke 4:18^E)

Jesus called those who were spiritually burdened to come to him.

> Come to me, *all you who are weary and burdened, and I will give you rest.* Take my yoke upon you and learn from me, for I am gentle and humble in heart, and you will find rest for your souls. For my yoke is easy and my burden is light." (Matt. 11:28–30^E)

"Blessed are those who mourn"—*Those who are repentant of their life condition*

There are many causes for mourning in our broken world. However, in the context of this prayer, mourning for personal sinfulness would certainly be significant. As previously noted, Jesus' first public proclamation was a call for *repentance* for wrongdoing. Jesus went into Galilee, proclaiming the good news of God:

> The time has come . . . the kingdom of God has come near. *Repent and believe the good news!* (Mark 1:14–15^E)

The response of some of those Jesus called into his presence was to *repent of social wrongdoing*. Such an occurrence is illustrated when Jesus passed through Jericho and encountered a wealthy tax collector named Zacchaeus.

In order to see Jesus, Zacchaeus climbed a tree. Jesus called Zacchaeus down and said that he would stay at his house. The crowd complained that Jesus had gone to be the guest of a sinner,

> But Zacchaeus stood up and said to the Lord, "Look, Lord! Here and now *I give half of my possessions to the poor, and if I have cheated anybody out of anything, I will pay back four times the amount.*" Jesus said to him, "Today salvation has come to this house, because this man, too, is a son of Abraham. For the Son of Man came to seek and to save the lost." (Luke 19:8–10[H])

"Blessed are the meek"—Those who are humble

Humility before God and others must be an attribute of those who follow Jesus. To those who were confident of their own righteousness and looked down upon others, Jesus told this parable:

> Two men went up to the temple to pray, one a Pharisee and the other a tax collector. The Pharisee stood by himself and prayed: "God, I thank you that I am not like other people—robbers, evildoers, adulterers—or even like this tax collector. I fast twice a week and give a tenth of all I get." But the tax collector stood at a distance. He would not even look up to heaven, but beat his breast and said, "God, have mercy on me, a sinner." I tell you that this man, rather than the other, went home justified before God. *For all those who exalt themselves will be humbled, and those who humble themselves will be exalted.* (Luke 18:10–14[H])

From Jesus' perspective, humility was a characteristic attitude in kingdom members.

He called a little child to him, and placed the child among them. And he said: "Truly I tell you, unless you change and become like little children, you will never enter the kingdom of heaven. Therefore, *whoever takes the lowly position of this child is the greatest in the kingdom of heaven*." (Matt. 18:2–4[H])

"Blessed are those who hunger and thirst for righteousness"

Jesus identified the pursuit of *God's righteousness on earth as the highest priority in his kingdom*. Jesus said:

> *But seek first* his kingdom and his righteousness, and all these things will be given to you as well. (Matt. 6:33[E])

This blessing moves from the personal to the communal context. The vocation of Jesus' followers is to promote God's right way of living in society. The remaining beatitudes and the further teaching in the Sermon on the Mount provide the details about righteous living.

"Blessed are the merciful"

Jesus' followers were to be merciful because they had received mercy from God. He illustrated this in a parable about an unmerciful servant, showing the close relationship between mercy and forgiveness. Jesus taught:

> Therefore, the kingdom of heaven is like a king who wanted to settle accounts with his servants. As he began the settlement, a man who owed him ten thousand bags of gold was brought to him. Since he was not able to pay, the master ordered that he and his wife and his children and all that he had be sold to repay the debt.

At this the servant fell on his knees before him. "Be patient with me," he begged, "and I will pay back everything." The servant's master took pity on him, canceled the debt and let him go. But when that servant went out, he found one of his fellow servants who owed him a hundred silver coins. He grabbed him and began to choke him. "Pay back what you owe me!" he demanded. His fellow servant fell to his knees and begged him, "Be patient with me, and I will pay it back." But he refused. Instead, he went off and had the man thrown into prison until he could pay the debt. When the other servants saw what had happened, they were outraged and went and told their master everything that had happened. Then the master called the servant in. "You wicked servant," he said, "I canceled all that debt of yours because you begged me to. *Shouldn't you have had mercy on your fellow servant just as I had on you?*" In anger his master handed him over to the jailers to be tortured, until he should pay back all he owed. This is how my heavenly Father will treat each of you unless you forgive your brother or sister from your heart. (Matt. 18:23–35[H])

As previously noted, forgiveness and mercy are foundational principles of living in God's kingdom. Jesus' cross is the symbol.

"Blessed are the pure in heart"—Those whose motivations are clean

Jesus' strongest condemnation was reserved for the hypocrisy of the Jewish religious leaders. These leaders claimed to know and do the will of God but they were far more concerned about their power and position in society. Kingdom values include "heart" motivations that are focused toward doing the will of God. The following is an example of Jesus' scathing criticism of religious hypocrisy.

> Woe to you, teachers of the law and Pharisees, you hypocrites! You are like whitewashed tombs, which look beautiful on the outside but on the inside are full of the bones of the dead and everything unclean. In the same way, on the outside you appear to people as righteous but on the inside you are full of hypocrisy and wickedness. (Matt. 23:27–28[1])

"Blessed are the peacemakers"

It is God's will that Jesus' followers seek peace, be peacemakers, except in the opposition to evil. Be reminded of the invocation to show mercy. Jesus' teachings about non-retaliation were among his most challenging. Peacemaking, where possible, is a kingdom attribute.

However, Jesus recognized that peace was not always possible to achieve. His presence on earth was a declaration of war against the powers of evil. The beatitude that comes next, about the expected persecution of his followers, acknowledges that complete peace cannot be achieved on earth. Jesus quotes from the prophet Micah to indicate that his teaching will even divide families.

> Do not suppose that I have come to bring peace to the earth. I did not come to bring peace, but a sword. For I have come to turn "a man against his father, a daughter against her mother, a daughter-in-law against her mother-in-law." (Matt. 10:34–35[E], quoting Mic. 7:6)
>
> You have heard that it was said, "Love your neighbor and hate your enemy." But I tell you, love your enemies

and pray for those who persecute you, *that you may be children of your Father in heaven.* He causes his sun to rise on the evil and the good, and sends rain on the righteous and the unrighteous. If you love those who love you, what reward will you get? Are not even the tax collectors doing that? And if you greet only your own people, what are you doing more than others? Do not even pagans do that? Be perfect, therefore, as your heavenly Father is perfect. (Matt. 5:43–48^E)

In Jesus' earthly kingdom the good and bad exist together, and God provides for human beings that do both good and evil. As difficult as it is to understand, Jesus teaches that this reality is in God's plan and therefore must be respected. Jesus challenges his followers to go beyond the natural human behavior of loving those who love them, but to care for those who oppose them.

"Blessed are those who are persecuted because of righteousness"—Those who suffer for promoting God's righteousness

This blessing is very significant, and Jesus discussed it in the most detail.

Blessed are you when people insult you, persecute you and falsely say all kinds of evil against you because of me. Rejoice and be glad, because great is your reward in heaven, for in the same way they persecuted the prophets who were before you. (Matt. 5:11–12^E)

Jesus was very clear: anyone who speaks against sin will be opposed, and he was the prime example of this reality. Jesus loved the disciples, and the future suffering of his followers was very distressing to him personally.

> If the world hates you, keep in mind that it hated me first. If you belonged to the world, it would love you as its own. As it is, you do not belong to the world, but I have chosen you out of the world. That is why the world hates you. Remember what I told you: "A servant is not greater than his master." If they persecuted me, they will persecute you also. If they obeyed my teaching, they will obey yours also. They will treat you this way because of my name, for they do not know the one who sent me. If I had not come and spoken to them, they would not be guilty of sin; but now they have no excuse for their sin. Whoever hates me hates my Father as well. If I had not done among them the works no one else did, they would not be guilty of sin. As it is, they have seen, and yet they have hated both me and my Father. (John 15:18–24[1])

In summary, these Beatitudes have painted the broad picture of what it means for Jesus' followers to live out the will of God in his kingdom. They will recognize their spiritual poverty, repent, and be humble before God. They will seek God's righteousness as a pure motive with a forgiving, peaceable spirit. They will expect opposition as they expose evil, and some may suffer greatly.

The remainder of the Sermon on the Mount provides further instruction about the behaviors that should characterize citizens of Jesus' kingdom. Jesus begins by emphasizing that righteous living glorifies God and concludes by stating that those who hear his words and put them into practice, will have the most secure and fulfilled life.

Doing God's Will—Jesus' Detailed Instruction about Kingdom Living

As Jesus' teaching continued, he taught that his followers were to be like salt, permeating society in order to preserve it. Further, they were to show forth the light of God's truth by publicly witnessing to Jesus who is the "light of the world."

> You are the salt of the earth. But if the salt loses its saltiness, how can it be made salty again? . . . You are the light of the world. A town built on a hill cannot be hidden. Neither do people light a lamp and put it under a bowl. Instead, they put it on its stand, and it gives light to everyone in the house. In the same way, *let your light shine before others*, that they may see your good deeds and glorify your Father in heaven. (Matt. 5:13–16^E)

Next, Jesus emphasized the foundational nature of the Old Testament law as a guide to Christian behavior.

> Therefore, anyone who sets aside one of the least of these commands and teaches others accordingly will be called least in the kingdom of heaven, but whoever practices and teaches these commands will be called great in the kingdom of heaven. For I tell you that unless your righteousness surpasses that of the Pharisees and the teachers of the law, you will certainly not enter the kingdom of heaven. (Matt. 5:19–20^E)

The above teaching requires careful interpretation. Jesus endorsed *the Judaic moral law*, but he strongly opposed the hypocrisy and legalism that demanded strict adherence to ceremonial laws and traditions while ignoring the underlying humane purpose of the law. Beyond that, Jesus was making the point that *entry into the kingdom cannot possibly be achieved by law keeping*. As becomes evident in Jesus' subsequent teaching, full obedience to God's moral law is beyond human capacity. Jesus taught that entry into God's kingdom was only possible based on belief in God's gracious forgiveness mediated through himself.

For the remainder of the sermon (Matt. 5:21–7:8^E), Jesus gave a series of principles to teach that full adherence to the intent of the law went far beyond literal and legalistic obedience to the rabbinic teachings of the time. This very important collection of Jesus' teachings is summarized below by theme.

Anger and reconciliation:

> But I tell you that anyone who is angry with a brother or sister will be subject to judgment . . . go and be reconciled to them; then come and offer your gift [in front of the altar] (5:21–24)

Marriage:

> You have heard that it was said, "You shall not commit adultery." But I tell you that anyone who looks at a woman lustfully has already committed adultery with her in his heart. . . . I tell you that anyone who divorces his wife, except for sexual immorality, makes her the

victim of adultery, and anyone who marries a divorced woman commits adultery. (5:27–32)

Honesty:

But I tell you, do not swear an oath at all. . . . All you need to say is simply "Yes" or "No"; anything beyond this comes from the evil one. (5:34–37)

Non-retaliation:

If anyone slaps you on the right cheek, turn to them the other cheek also. . . . But I tell you, love your enemies and pray for them that persecute you. (5:39–44)

Charitable giving:

So when you give to the needy, . . . do not let your left hand know what your right hand is doing, so that your giving may be in secret. (6:2–4)

Earthly wealth versus lasting spiritual reward:

But store up for yourselves treasures in heaven, where moths and vermin do not destroy. For where your treasure is, there your heart will be also. (6:20–21)

Looking at that which is good:

If your eyes are healthy, your whole body will be full of light. (6:22)

Material gain versus the service of God:

> No one can serve two masters. You will hate the one and love the other. . . . You cannot serve both God and money. (6:24)

Priority of seeking God's righteous rule:

> But seek first his kingdom and his righteousness, and all these things will be given to you as well. (6:33)

Judging others:

> Why do you look at the speck of sawdust in your brother's eye and pay no attention to the plank in your own eye? (7:3)

Seeking God's provision:

> Ask and it will be given to you; seek and you will find; knock and the door will be opened to you. (7:7)

This series of instructions for living culminates with the well-known Golden Rule which was a practical application of the second great commandment, "Love your neighbor as yourself":

> *So in everything, do to others what you would have them do to you*, for this sums up the Law and the Prophets. (7:12)

Jesus again reminded the disciples that in God's will, the number who enter his kingdom will be relatively few and that not all who appear to be followers are genuine.

> Enter through the narrow gate. For wide is the gate and broad is the road that leads to destruction, and many enter through it. But small is the gate and narrow the road that leads to life, and only a few find it. (7:13–14)
>
> Watch out for false prophets. They come to you in sheep's clothing, but inwardly they are ferocious wolves. By their fruit you will recognize them. (7:15–16)
>
> Not everyone who says to me, "Lord, Lord," will enter the kingdom of heaven, but only the one who does the will of my Father who is in heaven. (7:21)

This compilation of Jesus' teaching concludes with a parable proclaiming that his teaching, put into practice, was the only solid foundation for building one's personal life.

> Therefore, *everyone who hears these words of mine and puts them into practice is like a wise man who built his house on the rock.* The rain came down, the streams rose, and the winds blew and beat against that house; yet it did not fall, because it had its foundation on the rock. But everyone who hears these words of mine and does not put them into practice is like a foolish man who built his house on sand. The rain came down, the streams rose, and the winds blew and beat against that house, and it fell with a great crash. (7:24–27)

In the Christian story, the fulfillment of the prayer that *God's will be done on earth* was committed to an unlikely group of disciples. It seems improbable, and yet, Jesus' kingdom has been sustained for two millennia and has permeated every part of the earth. Empowered by God's Spirit and guided by the Spirit-inspired Word of God, humble and repentant human beings have been motivated to pray for and to practice the righteous will of God in the world only by the power of God's Spirit.

Part Two

Our Physical and Spiritual Needs

6

The Fourth Petition: "Give Us Today Our Daily Bread"

This fourth petition begins a transition from focusing on God's name, kingdom, and will to addressing the physical and spiritual needs of those who follow Jesus. Many of the important occurrences and teachings in the gospel narratives are about food, such as the time Jesus' disciples were accused of picking corn on the Sabbath.

> At that time Jesus went through the grainfields on the Sabbath. His disciples were hungry and began to pick some heads of grain and eat them. When the Pharisees saw this, they said to him, "Look! Your disciples are doing what is unlawful on the Sabbath." He answered, "Haven't you read what David did when he and his companions were hungry? He entered the house of God, and he and his companions ate the consecrated bread—which was not lawful for them to do, but only for the priests." (Matt. 12:1–4^E)

Jesus placed the human need for food above the adherence to Jewish religious ritual.

The writers of the Gospels give many examples of Jesus' attention to the needs of people for food and drink. Jesus' *first miracle* was not a healing; it was to provide wine at a wedding. It was not for necessity but for social pleasure.

> A wedding took place at Cana in Galilee. Jesus' mother was there, and Jesus and his disciples had also been invited to the wedding. When the wine was gone, Jesus' mother said to him, "They have no more wine." "Woman, why do you involve me?" Jesus replied. "My hour has not yet come." His mother said to the servants, "Do whatever he tells you."
>
> Nearby stood six stone water jars, the kind used by the Jews for ceremonial washing, each holding from twenty to thirty gallons.
>
> Jesus said to the servants, "Fill the jars with water;" so they filled them to the brim.
>
> Then he told them, "Now draw some out and take it to the master of the banquet."
>
> They did so, and the master of the banquet tasted the water that had been turned into wine. He did not realize where it had come from, though the servants who had drawn the water knew. Then he called the bridegroom aside and said, "Everyone brings out the choice wine first and then the cheaper wine after the guests have had too much to drink; but you have saved the best till now." What Jesus did here in Cana of Galilee was the first of the signs through which he revealed his glory; and his disciples believed in him. (John 2:1–11[D])

During his itinerant teaching, Jesus often demonstrated his understanding of the people's need for food. This concern for the needs of those he was teaching was the reason for a miracle of feeding thousands.

> Then Jesus went up on a mountainside and sat down with his disciples. The Jewish Passover Festival was near. When Jesus looked up and saw a great crowd coming toward him, he said to Philip, "Where shall we buy bread for these people to eat?" He asked this only to test him, for he already had in mind what he was going to do. (John 6:4–6^G).

Jesus then miraculously fed the crowd, using only a few loaves and fishes.

Dependence on God for Provision for Our Lives

This petition, "give us today our daily bread," is about more than the provision of food; it is about God's provision for all the physical needs of our lives. It indicates that Jesus intended this to be a *daily* prayer. Daily prayerful communication with God is essential to a meaningful relationship. It is also important not to be too confident about our own ability to provide for ourselves. Daily prayer for our needs is a helpful reminder of our continuing reliance on God's provision, which Jesus illustrated with the following story:

> The ground of a certain rich man yielded an abundant harvest. He thought to himself, "What shall I do? I have no place to store my crops." Then he said, "This is what I'll do. I will tear down my barns and build bigger ones, and there I will store my surplus grain. And I'll say to myself, "You have plenty of grain laid up for many years. Take life easy; eat, drink and be merry." But God said to him, "You fool! This very night your life will be demanded from you. Then who will get what you have prepared for yourself?"

> This is how it will be with whoever stores up things for themselves but is not rich toward God. (Luke 12:16–21[H])

Responsibility of Jesus' Followers to Care for the Needs of Others

The words "*our* daily bread" inform the Christian concern that everyone be given the necessities of life. From the time of the early church until our time, Christians and Christian missions have been in the forefront of providing food, water, shelter, and clothing for those in need. Recall the words of Jesus as he commanded his followers to aid the destitute,

> For I was hungry and you gave me something to eat, I was thirsty and you gave me something to drink, I was a stranger and you invited me in, I needed clothes and you clothed me, I was sick and you looked after me, I was in prison and you came to visit me. . . . Truly I tell you, whatever you did for one of the least of these brothers and sisters of mine, you did for me. (Matt. 25:35, 40[I])

This forceful statement is a clear indication that providing for the needs of others for nourishment, clothing, and shelter is a basic commitment for members of Jesus' kingdom. Jesus identified such acts of giving to others as giving to him personally. Again, we are reminded that love of God is demonstrated through love of neighbor. The Christian story teaches us that, ultimately, we are reliant on God for our physical needs, but it also commits us to attend to the needs of others.

7

The Fifth Petition: "Forgive Us Our Debts, as We Also Have Forgiven Our Debtors"

God's Forgiveness of Us

The essential message of the Christian story is about God's loving forgiveness of our sins / debts. The memorial that Jesus established for himself was the Eucharist, taking bread and wine, representing his body broken and blood shed on the cross for *the forgiveness of sin*.

> This is my blood of the covenant, which is poured out for many *for the forgiveness of sins*. (Matt. 26:28[1])

Again, be reminded of the words of Jesus toward the end of his earthly life:

> The Messiah will suffer and rise from the dead on the third day, and *repentance for the forgiveness of sins* will be preached in his name to all nations. (Luke 24:46–47[L])

The death of Jesus, for the forgiveness of our sin, was the ultimate demonstration of God's love for humankind.

The apostle Paul wrote about the great mystery of God's forgiveness through the death of Jesus:

> [God] did not spare his own Son, but gave him up for us all. (Rom. 8:32)

Jesus' death was filled with immense suffering, betrayal by friends, trial by Roman authorities, mocking by soldiers, and cruel crucifixion. His suffering becomes very evident in his words before, and while on, the cross:

> They went to a place called Gethsemane. . . . He fell to the ground and prayed that, if possible, the hour might pass from him. "*Abba* Father, he said, everything is possible for you. Take this cup from me. Yet not what I will, but what you will." (Mark 14:32–36[J])
>
> It was nine in the morning when they crucified him. . . . Jesus cried out in a loud voice . . . "My God, my God, why have you forsaken me?" (Mark 15:25, 34[K])

Our need for forgiveness is made evident in our human lives by the emotion of guilt, "a feeling of deserving blame for offenses."[15] Guilt arises when humans recognize that their actions have done harm to others. The great philosopher Immanuel Kant affirmed this reality in a statement that became inscribed on his tombstone:

> Two things fill the mind with ever new and increasing admiration and awe, the more often and steadily we reflect upon them: the starry heavens above me and *the moral law* within me.[16]

From the Christian perspective, "the moral law within" is a God-imparted human attribute. Throughout human history this moral sense has found many different understandings and expressions in various cultures and subcultures. The message of Jesus is rooted in the Judaic understanding of the righteousness of God and the sinfulness of humankind.

The biblical story began in the book of Genesis with a description of the sin and guilt of the earliest human beings who disobeyed God and wronged their fellows. It continued in the subsequent books of the Old Testament with the establishment of God's laws to protect society and to punish those who disobey. The best known of these laws are the Ten Commandments, delivered through Moses (Exodus 20:1–17; appendix 3). In the Christian story, "sin" is the human failure to honor God and his creation. Human beings were made in the "image of God" (Gen. 1:26). Both the Ten Commandments and Jesus' Great Commandment join the worship and love of God with right behavior toward others. The most obvious manifestation of sin in our world is the tragic disrespect for and destruction of our fellow human beings.

However, the life and teaching of Jesus exposed the deep root of sin as being human *pride and the rejection of God*. The religious leaders rejected, and ultimately crucified, God's Son because of the threat he posed to their proudly held positions and traditions. Jesus told his disciples that, after he left the earth, the Spirit of God would come and show the world that the rejection of God's Son was the primary sin. Jesus taught,

> It is for your good that I am going away. Unless I go away the Advocate will not come to you; but if I go away, I will send him to you. When he comes, he will prove the world to be wrong about sin and righteousness and judgment: *about sin because the people do not believe in me.* (John 16:7–9[1])

At a personal level, praying this petition for forgiveness is an act of confession. We pray that God's will be done, but we recognize that we can never fully live up to God's standards, and so we pray, "forgive us our debts."

As an example of God's forgiveness, Jesus demonstrated remarkable forgiveness for his disciple Peter, as shown in the following sequence of events. Before Jesus was placed on trial, he taught his disciples that he would suffer.

> Simon Peter asked him, "Lord, where are you going?" Jesus replied, "Where I am going, you cannot follow now, but you will follow later." Peter asked, "Lord, why can't I follow you now? I will lay down my life for you." Then Jesus answered, "Will you really lay down your life for me? Very truly I tell you, before the rooster crows, you will disown me three times!" (John 13:36–38[1])

A few hours later, while Peter was observing Jesus' trial before the Jewish authorities, he denied that he knew Jesus three times. As Peter stood in the room a servant girl asked him,

> "You aren't one of this man's disciples too, are you?" she asked Peter. He replied, "*I am not.*" . . . Simon Peter was still standing there warming himself. So they asked

him, You aren't one of his disciples too, are you?" He denied it, saying, "*I am not.*" One of the high priest's servants, a relative of the man whose ear Peter had cut off, challenged him, "Didn't I see you with him in the garden?" *Again, Peter denied it,* and at that moment a rooster began to crow. (John 18:17– 27[J])

After Jesus had risen, he came to some of the disciples, including Peter, at the lakeshore where they had been fishing. When they came to shore, they had breakfast with Jesus and he addressed Peter.

> Jesus said to Simon Peter, "Simon, son of John, do you love me more than these?" "Yes, Lord," he said, "you know that I love you." Jesus said, "*Feed my lambs.*" Again, Jesus said, "Simon son of John, do you love me?" He answered, "Yes, Lord, you know that I love you." Jesus said, "*Take care of my sheep.*" The third time he said to him, "Simon, son of John, do you love me?" Peter was hurt because Jesus asked him the third time, "Do you love me?" He said, "Lord, you know all things; you know that I love you." Jesus said, "*Feed my sheep.*" ... Then he said to him, "Follow me!" (John 21:15–19[L])

Three times Peter denied that he knew Jesus, and three times Jesus showed his forgiveness to Peter and reinstated him to become a major leader in the early Christian movement.

Jesus' greatest act of forgiveness to those who reject him was witnessed as he was being crucified.

> While in agony on the cross, Jesus called out, exclaiming, Father, forgive them, for they do not know what they are doing. (Luke 23:34[K]).

In summary, the gospel, the good news, of Jesus is not a message of defeat or despair. The emphasis of the Christian story is that of *God's gracious forgiveness*, based on Jesus' sacrificial death. Forgiveness of sin, through Jesus, is the Christian's source of joy and hope.

Our Forgiveness of Others

The phrase "as we also have forgiven our debtors" has been the cause of much discussion among Christian writers. Does this statement imply contingency to God's forgiveness of sinners? Jesus gave very strong emphasis to this petition because the teaching, immediately following his prayer, was focussed on forgiveness of others.

> For if you forgive other people when they sin against you, your heavenly Father will also forgive you. But if you do not forgive others their sins, your Father will not forgive your sins. (Matt. 6:14–15[E])

Darryl Johnson states that Martin Luther was one who maintained "a one-to-one correspondence between our forgiving others and our being forgiven by God."[17] Alexander Maclaren, a great Scottish preacher of the late 1800s, calls this phrase "the startling addition to the prayer." He continues,

> Is, then, our poor forgiveness the measure or condition of God's? At sight that addition seems to impose a limit on his pardon which might well plunge us into despair. But reflection on the words brings to light more comforting, though solemnly warning, thoughts.

> ... In a very real sense, our forgiving is the condition of our being forgiven. We are accustomed to hear that faith and repentance are conditions of receiving the divine forgiveness. But the very same disposition which, when directed to God, produces faith and repentance, when directed to men, produces a forgiving temper. A deep sense of my own unworthiness, and of having no ground of right to stand on, will surely lead me to be lenient and forgiving of others. We cannot cut our lives into halves, and be inwardly filled with contrition, and outwardly full of assertion of our rights. We cannot plead with God to do for us what we will not do for others. Our prayer for forgiveness must, if it is real, influence our whole behavior; and if it is not real, it will not be answered.[18]

From this perspective, forgiveness of others is not a precondition for forgiveness but evidence of true repentance. Jesus taught that being a member of his kingdom was always a communitarian proposition, not private religion. Just as the phrase "*our* daily bread" implies physical sharing, so the phrase "have forgiven *our* debtors" implies spiritual sharing. Forgiveness is the deepest expression of God's love and therefore will characterize the lives of Jesus' followers. Jesus taught this principle and stressed the importance of forgiving others on several occasions. One example is when

> Peter came to Jesus and asked, "Lord, how many times shall I forgive my brother or sister who sins against me? Up to seven times?" Jesus answered, "I tell you, not seven times, but seventy-seven times." (Matt. 18:21–22[H])

And he taught his disciples,

> Do not judge, and you will not be judged. Do not condemn, and you will not be condemned. Forgive, and you will be forgiven. (Luke 6:37[F])

Again, note that Christian living is always aspirational. Jesus' cross is the symbol of full forgiveness and supersedes all human sin, including human inability to fully forgive. Jesus' followers will pray daily for forgiveness of our debts and be reminded of our obligation to forgive those who have wronged us.

God's forgiveness is a gift; it is not a "free pass" to continue sinning or to not make restitution for previous offences. Jesus taught,

> Therefore, if you are offering your gift at the altar and there remember that your brother or sister has something against you, leave your gift there in front of the altar. First go and be reconciled to them; then come and offer your gift. (Matt. 5:23–24[E])

In summary, the foremost message of the Christian story is about restoring right relationships with God and one another. Praying this petition recognizes the need for personal forgiveness and the responsibility to forgive others. Praying to God for forgiveness (i.e., repentance) is the first step into the Christian story.

8

The Sixth Petition: "Lead Us Not into Temptation"

This petition is a natural outflow from the prayer that God will forgive our debts. If we truly ask for forgiveness, it makes sense to ask God to help us not to incur further debts. It is a cry from the heart, acknowledging our human weakness and expressing our desire to live out the will of God. Jesus made a well-known comment about this serious problem when he took Peter, James, and John to pray with him before he was crucified. They fell asleep. Jesus said to them,

> Watch and pray so you will not fall into temptation. *The spirit is willing, but the flesh is weak.* (Matt. 26:40[J])

As if to prove the point, the disciples fell asleep again.

There has been much theological discussion about the idea that God could lead his followers into temptation. John Stott suggests that "lead us not into temptation but deliver us from the evil one" should be considered together since it is "the evil one" who does the tempting.[19] In the example of Jesus' temptation, God's Spirit led Jesus into the wilderness but the temptation came from Satan.

Then Jesus was led by the Spirit into the wilderness to be tempted by the devil. After fasting forty days and forty nights, he was hungry. The tempter came to him and said, "If you are the Son of God, tell these stones to become bread." Jesus answered, "It is written: 'Man shall not live on bread alone, but on every word that comes from the mouth of God.'" Then the devil took him to the holy city and had him stand on the highest point of the temple. "If you are the Son of God," he said, "throw yourself down. For it is written: 'He will command his angels concerning you, and they will lift you up in their hands, so that you will not strike your foot against a stone.'" Jesus answered him, *"It is also written: 'Do not put the Lord your God to the test.'"* Again, the devil took him to a very high mountain and showed him all the kingdoms of the world and their splendor. "All this I will give you," he said, "if you will bow down and worship me." Jesus said to him, "Away from me, Satan! For it is written: 'Worship the Lord your God, and serve him only.'" Then the devil left him, and angels came and attended him. (Matt. 4:1–11^C)

The temptations Jesus endured were temptations to be diverted from his mission as the redeemer of humankind

- by giving higher priority to physical wants than the need for hearing God,
- by testing God's power for personal affirmation, and
- by giving allegiance to the devil in order to gain riches and power.

Jesus encountered another temptation from Satan through his disciple Peter.

> Jesus began to explain to his disciples that he must go to Jerusalem and suffer many things at the hands of the elders, the chief priests and the teachers of the law, and that he must be killed and on the third day be raised to life. Peter took him aside and began to rebuke him. "Never, Lord!" he said. "This shall never happen to you!" Jesus turned and said to Peter, "Get behind me, Satan! *You are a stumbling block to me*; you do not have in mind the concerns of God, but merely human concerns." (Matt. 16:21–23ᴳ)

Peter's very human reaction of concern must have reminded Jesus of the temptation he received from Satan in the wilderness, the temptation to abandon his mission. It is an example of how temptations from the evil one can come from unexpected sources.

Temptations abound in our lives; they change with age and circumstances. The logical step after praying daily for forgiveness is to pray to be kept from unrighteous attitudes and actions. Therefore, even if we may not understand the dynamics, it is appropriate to pray that God will "lead us not into temptation." Rather, as is written in the well-known Psalm 23, we should pray that God will lead us "along the right paths for his namesake" (v. 3).

The writer of the book of Hebrews states an overriding principle in the Christian story: even as we will be tempted, Jesus is able to understand and forgive our weaknesses.

For we do not have a high priest who is unable to empathize with our weaknesses, but we have one who has been tempted in every way, just as we are—yet he did not sin. (4:15)

9

The Seventh Petition: "Deliver Us from the Evil One"

This final petition, "but deliver us from the evil one," is a fitting conclusion to the prayer. Deliverance of individuals and society from the evil one was the purpose of Jesus and his followers. This petition is relevant in Jesus' kingdom both at the present and in the future, final deliverance.

Jesus dealt with the reality of evil and the evil one, but he never taught about the ultimate origins of evil. Jesus did not teach that evil events were punishments for sin. He saw the world, including good and evil, as the *template* against which God's purposes were to be fulfilled. In fact, as exemplified by Jesus' healing ministry and his crucifixion, evil became the context in which God's love was shown.

On one occasion, as Jesus was about to heal a blind man, he taught his disciples:

> As he went along, he saw a man blind from birth. His disciples asked him, "Rabbi, who sinned, this man or his parents, that he was born blind?" "*Neither this man nor his parents sinned,*" *said Jesus,* "but this happened so that the works of God might be displayed in him. As

long as it is day, we must do the works of him who sent me. Night is coming, when no one can work. While I am in the world, I am the light of the world." (John 9:1–5[H])

On another occasion Jesus was asked whether some men were killed by a natural disaster because they had sinned. Jesus replied,

> Those eighteen who died when the tower in Siloam fell on them—do you think they were more guilty than all the others living in Jerusalem? I tell you, no! But unless you repent, you too will all perish. (Luke 13:4–5[H])

Professor N. T. Wright was quoted in *Time* magazine concerning evil in the context of the Covid-19 pandemic. He writes that the Christian response to evil is lament, *not explanation*.

> Lament is what happens when people ask "Why?" and don't get an answer. . . . It is not part of the Christian vocation to explain what is happening and why. . . . In the Bible, God laments. . . . As the Spirit laments within us, so we become small shrines where the healing love of God can dwell. And out of that can emerge new acts of kindness, new scientific understanding, and new hope.[20]

As has been discussed, Jesus was delivered from the temptations and assaults of "the evil one" until he chose to be crucified. Jesus was delivered finally from "the evil one" by his resurrection. Jesus' ministry on earth involved delivering his contemporaries from evil through his teaching and healing. In Jesus' day, much illness was attributed to "the evil one," and on several occasions Jesus' miracles were described as casting out demons.

Today, many of the physical, bacteriological, and molecular causes of such described disorders have been identified. However, this does not obviate the evil of illness and death. Jesus' encounters with the demons are not normative in our time. However, we can take direction from him and join in his attack on the evils of sickness, death, and injustice. This mission has been undertaken by Christians over the centuries. The significant role of Christians in the rise of health care, education, and law has had a profound impact on civilization.

At the beginning of creation, God proclaimed the human purpose: to "increase in number; fill the earth and subdue it" (Gen. 1:28). Overcoming evil and harm and doing good is the God-given mandate. This was exemplified in everything Jesus did and should characterize the lives of his followers in their life choices and actions.

Jesus was particularly concerned that his followers be protected from the evil one after he had left the earth. In some of Jesus' last words to his disciples, he prayed to the Father,

> I have given them your word and the world has hated them, for they are not of the world any more than I am of the world. My prayer is not that you take them out of the world but that *you protect them from the evil one*. They are not of the world, even as I am not of it. Sanctify them by the truth; your word is truth. As you sent me into the world, I have sent them into the world. (John 17:14–18[1])

From a human perspective, deliverance from evil is the ultimate purpose of the Christian story. This delivery from evil was foreshadowed in Genesis, the earliest chapters of the Old Testament, and dramatically described in Revelation, the last book of the New Testament. Jesus taught that the hope of resurrection from the dead and eternal life would be the final delivery from evil for those who follow him.

> Do not let your hearts be troubled. You believe in God; believe also in me. My Father's house has many rooms; if that were not so, would I have told you that I am going there to prepare a place for you? And if I go and prepare a place for you, I will come back and take you to be with me that you also may be where I am. (John 14:1–3[1])

The Christian Story has no ending.

10

Matthew's Closing (KJV*): "For Thine Is the Kingdom, and the Power, and the Glory, for Ever"

This traditional ending of the Lord's Prayer is taken from the early seventeenth-century King James translation of the Bible*. There is scholarly debate on whether these words of praise were included in the original manuscripts, and they have been excluded from modern Protestant translations. These words are a doxology, likely derived from the praise to God offered by David, the Jewish king.

> Yours, LORD, is the greatness and the power and the glory and the majesty and the splendor, for everything in heaven and earth is yours. Yours, LORD, is the kingdom. (1 Chron. 29:11)

Jesus may have said this, and it certainly reflects the worship of the early Christians who experienced the life changing power of God through Jesus Christ. As the apostle Paul wrote to the Christian community in the city of Ephesus,

> I pray that the eyes of your heart may be enlightened in order that you may know the hope to which God has called you, the riches of his glorious inheritance in his holy people, and his incomparably great power for us who believe. That power is the same as the mighty strength he exerted when he raised Christ from the dead and seated him at his right hand in the heavenly realms, far above all rule and authority, power and dominion, and every name that is invoked, not only in the present age but also in the one to come. (Eph. 1:18–21)

Afterword

This writing began with the premise that the Christian Bible contains a grand story about the meaning of life and the best way to live it. In his book *Becoming C. S. Lewis*, Harry Lee Poe described how Lewis, the renowned writer and professor of English literature, became a Christian when he realized that the Christian story was exceptional among such stories, whether ancient sagas or modern philosophies.[21] The Christian story was *God's story*, told as only God could tell it, *written into history*, culminating in the life, death, and resurrection of his Son, Jesus of Nazareth. Lewis is an example of the multitude for whom the Christian story has become the ultimate source of meaning and joy in life.

These *Notes* have explored the Christian story through the words of Jesus using the petitions of the Lord's Prayer as a guide. Those who live in the Christian story are challenged to pray each day that

- God's loving and just character will be honored and demonstrated,
- Jesus' kingdom of love and justice will be established and expand on earth,
- Jesus' followers will display and promote God's righteous will,
- God will provide for our physical needs and for the needs of others,
- God will forgive us and that we will be forgiving of others,

- God will keep us from temptation and unrighteous behaviors, and
- God will protect us from evil as we seek to combat evil in this world.

By praying and living out Jesus' prayer, those who inhabit the Christian story become participants with Jesus' Spirit in bringing the Father's kingdom of life and light into the world.

Amen.

Appendix 1

The Creeds

Apostles' Creed

I believe in God, the Father Almighty, Maker of heaven and earth.

And in Jesus Christ, his only begotten Son, our Lord; who was conceived by the Holy Spirit, born of the Virgin Mary, suffered under Pontius Pilate, was crucified, died, and was buried.

He descended into hell. On the third day he rose from the dead; He ascended into heaven, and sits at the right hand of God the Father Almighty; from there he shall come again to judge the living and the dead.

I believe in the Holy Spirit, the holy catholic church, the communion of saints, the forgiveness of sins, the resurrection of the body, and the life everlasting. Amen.

Nicene Creed

We believe in one God, the Father, the Almighty, maker of heaven and earth, of all that is, seen and unseen.

We believe in one Lord, Jesus Christ, the only Son of God, eternally begotten of the Father, God from God,

Light from Light, true God from true God, begotten, not made, of one being with the Father. Through him all things were made.

For us and for our salvation he came down from heaven; by the power of the Holy Spirit, he became incarnate of the Virgin Mary, and was made man.

For our sake he was crucified under Pontius Pilate; he suffered death and was buried. On the third day he rose again in accordance with the scriptures; he ascended into heaven and is seated at the right hand of the father.

He will come again in glory to judge the living and the dead, and his kingdom will have no end. We believe in the Holy Spirit, the Lord, the giver of life, who proceeds from the Father and the Son. With the Father and the Son he is worshipped and glorified. He has spoken through the Prophets.

We believe in one holy catholic and apostolic Church. We acknowledge one baptism for the forgiveness of sins. We look for the resurrection of the dead, and the life of the world to come. Amen.

Appendix 2

The Story of Jesus' Life

> [Jesus] was born some 20 centuries ago to an impoverished couple in an obscure part of the planet. Only several thousand people interacted with him. He never traveled outside his region. He didn't write a book. He didn't have a home. The Romans didn't consider him significant enough to record his execution in their records. Jesus stepped into a world with a rigid religious establishment, a pagan empire and political parties of all stripes. Normally at odds with each other, these powers conspired to literally take Jesus out. (Attributed to Dr. Michael Sprague)

This cogent description will serve as an introduction to this brief summary of the life of Jesus as recorded in the Four Gospels of the New Testament, Matthew, Mark, Luke, and John.

Jesus was born in Palestine, probably around 6 to 4 BCE. He was born in the town of Bethlehem and grew up in Nazareth, in the area of Galilee, about one hundred and fifty kilometers north of Jerusalem. Little is known about Jesus' early life, except for one glimpse when his parents took him to Jerusalem at the age of twelve. They found

Jesus in the temple courts, sitting among the teachers, listening to them and asking them questions. Everyone who heard him was amazed at his understanding and his answers (Luke 2:46–47[B]).

Jesus was called the son of a carpenter, and is thought to have followed his father's trade.

> Isn't this the carpenter's son? Isn't his mother's name Mary, and aren't his brothers James, Joseph, Simon and Judas? (Matt. 13:55[F])

The language Jesus spoke in his home would have been Aramaic, but given his use of the Old Testament, Jesus knew the Hebrew Scriptures and possibly some Greek.

Jesus began his public itinerant ministry at about thirty years of age. (Luke 3:23)

> Jesus went throughout Galilee, teaching in their synagogues, proclaiming the good news of the kingdom, and healing every disease and sickness among the people. (Matt. 4:23[E])

During the time of his ministry, Jesus' travels spanned from Galilee, an area surrounding the Lake of Tiberius (Sea of Galilee) in the north of Palestine, to Jerusalem and the surrounding area called Judea, less than two hundred kilometers to the south. At this time, Palestine was under Roman domination. The country was ruled first by the Roman vassal king Herod the Great, who was a practicing Jew. After Herod's death, the area administrators included Antipas and Pilate. Pilate governed from 26 to 36 CE and presided over Jesus' crucifixion.

There were three major Jewish religious groups, the Pharisees, Sadducees, and temple priests. Pharisaic Judaism was focused on strict obedience to the law and was based in synagogues located throughout the country. The Sadducees were the wealthy upper class whose lives were much involved with the Jerusalem temple worship that was conducted by the priests. Jesus was particularly critical of the Pharisees who were a movement that placed great emphasis on the purity code but were hypocritical and unloving. Jesus' teaching and miracles threatened all the religious powers of the time.

The Gospels are thought to be written between thirty to seventy years after Jesus' life. They were intended to provide the expanding Christian churches with definitive documentation about Jesus' life and teaching. The gospels of Mark and Luke were most likely authored by travel companions of the apostle Paul and associates of the apostle Peter. Both would have known many of Jesus' first disciples and other principals in the early Christian story, from whom they could obtain and transcribe eyewitness information.

Mark's Gospel was probably the first biography of Jesus and was focused on the dramatic entry of God's kingdom into the world through Jesus. Much of the information in Mark's Gospel is also found in Luke and Matthew.

Luke gave a description of why and how he composed his gospel. He suggests that there were "many" written accounts about Jesus at the time and that his collation brought them together into an orderly document.

> Many have undertaken to draw up an account of the things that have been fulfilled among us, just as

they were handed down to us by those who from the first were eyewitnesses and servants of the word. With this in mind, since I myself have carefully investigated everything from the beginning, I too decided to write an orderly account for you, most excellent Theophilus, so that you may know the certainty of the things you have been taught. (Luke 1:1–4)

The Gospel of Matthew is focused on a Jewish Christian audience. Its contents are derived from several sources, many shared with Mark, some with Luke. This Gospel includes significant information that is not found in the other gospels, such as the most complete version of the Sermon on the Mount. Though the gospel was named after one of Jesus' disciples, it is thought likely to have been compiled by another scribe.

John's Gospel is thought to be the last one written. It is different from the other gospels—more philosophical and highly selective. This gospel contributes substantial intimate insight, including detailed descriptions of Jesus' encounters with individuals, significant miracles, and lengthy quotations of Jesus' teaching to his disciples during his last days on earth. These facts suggest that the author was John, the "beloved" disciple (John 13:23), or a close associate. The Gospel of John was written for a very specific purpose:

> that you may believe that Jesus is the Messiah, the son of God, and that by believing you may have life in his name. (20:31)

Most of what we know about Jesus is recorded in the New Testament, in what are termed the four "canonical gospels." Other writings about Jesus' life did circulate in the early Christian context, but these were not accepted by the church councils as worthy of inclusion in the cannon of scriptures. There are some references to Jesus made by historians, after his death, that confirm his existence.[22]

Since the eighteenth century, because the gospel records were not entirely parallel and many of the stories recorded were not compatible with scientific understandings, numerous attempts have been made to identify a "historical Jesus" that conformed to current understandings. There has been little consensus in such efforts. As in these *Notes*, most Christians accept the Four Gospels to be Spirit inspired and to convey the essential message of the gospel. For example, the recorded miracles of Jesus were often a dramatization of spiritual truth and therefore an important aspect of his message.

Jesus is thought to have lived for about thirty-three years. In the later part of his life, his public teaching and healing ministry probably lasted for three and a half years. There have been many scholarly discussions about the timing or events in Jesus' life. For the purpose of this writing, the following is a proposed sequential outline of the story of Jesus' life, death, and resurrection as recorded in the Four Gospels and the book of Acts. I am particularly grateful for the on-line, accessible *The Walk with the Word: Parallel Gospels*, prepared by D. E. Isom.[23] Also, *The New Testament in Its World*, by N. T. Wright and Michael F. Bird,[24] has been very helpful.

Since the Gospels contain different material, this account of the story is arranged in segments, A to L, in order to identify a likely time period and location of Jesus' words as quoted in these *Notes*.

A. Before Jesus' Birth—Luke 1:5–80; Matthew 1:18–25

Luke begins telling Jesus' story by describing the circumstances around the birth of his relative, John the Baptist. John became the prophetic forerunner when Jesus emerged as a teacher and healer. Next, Luke describes that an angel appeared to Mary, Jesus' mother to be, to inform her about her future son, saying,

> He will be great and will be called the Son of the Most High. (Luke 1:32)

Matthew begins by stating that Jesus was to be born of a virgin named Mary. He relates Jesus' birth to a prophecy from the Old Testament:

> Therefore, the Lord himself will give you a sign: The virgin will conceive and give birth to a son, and will call him Immanuel. (Isa. 7:14)

Subsequently, an angel appeared to Joseph, who was to become Mary's husband, to reassure him.

B. Jesus' Birth and Youth—Luke 2:1–52; Matthew 2:1–23

According to Luke, Joseph and Mary travelled from their home in the town of Nazareth to Bethlehem for the purpose of a census. While in Bethlehem, Jesus was born.

Shepherds, working nearby, were alerted to Jesus' birth by angels, who told them,

> Today in the town of David, a Savior has been born to you; he is the Messiah, the Lord. (Luke 2:11)

Eight days after Jesus' birth, he was presented at the temple for circumcision. Again, Jesus' presence was accompanied by prophecy from Simeon who exclaimed,

> My eyes have seen your salvation. (Luke 2:30)

In the same time frame, Matthew told of Magi from the east who, based on astrology and a unique star, came to find "one born king of the Jews" and worship him with gifts (Matt. 2:2). Herod the Tetrarch became aware of this event and, being threatened, arranged to have the infant boys in the area killed. However, Joseph and Mary had been forewarned by an angel and fled to Egypt. Years later, the family returned to Nazareth in Galilee.

The next encounter with Jesus is recorded by Luke. At the age of twelve, Jesus had travelled with his parents to Jerusalem and was found in the temple conversing with the teachers who were reported to be amazed by his understanding. As Jesus' life continued in Nazareth, it is written,

> And Jesus grew in wisdom and stature, and in favor with God and man. (Luke 2:52)

C. Baptism and Temptation of Jesus—Mark 1:1–13; Matthew 3:1–4:11; Luke 3:1–4:13

Mark's Gospel begins with Jesus in his early thirties. John the Baptist had come to the Judean countryside "preaching a baptism of repentance" (v. 4). Jesus was in the area. Mark records Jesus' baptism by John the Baptist who announced that Jesus was "the Son of God." Matthew and Luke also describe Jesus' baptism, followed by accounts of Jesus going into the wilderness to be tempted by Satan.

D. The Beginning of Jesus Public Ministry—John 1:19-4:42

In John's Gospel, the story of Jesus begins with the appearance of John the Baptist, who preached repentance to crowds in the Judean wilderness. He proclaimed Jesus to be "the Lamb of God" (1:29). John's Gospel alludes to Jesus' baptism followed by an account of Jesus calling his first disciples, Andrew, Simon Peter, Philip, and Nathanael. Jesus and these followers returned to Galilee where Jesus performed his first public miracle, turning water into wine.

Jesus then walked back to Jerusalem where John records an episode of Jesus chasing money changers from the temple. Jesus then met with a Jewish leader, Nicodemus, with whom he discussed the need for "new birth" and predicted his death on a cross. Jesus and the disciples returned to Galilee through Samaria, where Jesus engaged in a profound discussion with a Samaritan woman about the true nature of worship.

E. Jesus' Return to Galilee—Matthew 4:12-12:48; Mark 1:14-3:12; Luke 4:14-6:11; John 4:43-54

The Four Gospels follow Jesus back to Galilee. Matthew writes,

> Jesus went throughout Galilee, teaching in their synagogues, proclaiming the good news of the kingdom, and healing every disease and sickness among the people. News about him spread all over Syria, and people brought to him all who were ill with various diseases, those suffering severe pain, the demon-possessed, those having seizures, and the paralyzed; and he healed them. Large crowds from Galilee, the Decapolis, Jerusalem, Judea, and the region across the Jordan followed him. (Matt. 4:23–25)

Luke records Jesus' first teaching in the Nazareth synagogue where Jesus proclaimed himself to be the fulfillment of Isaiah's prophecy (Isa. 61:1–2). In Galilee, Jesus called more disciples, travelled widely, performed many healings, and gave much significant teaching. Of note, Matthew contains a large compilation of Jesus' teaching in the Sermon on the Mount (5:1–7:28).

F. *The Second Year of Jesus' Ministry—Matthew 13:1–14:12; Mark 3:13–6:29; Luke 6:12–9:9; John 5:1–47*

Matthew, Mark, and Luke contain most of the information about Jesus' second year of public ministry. Jesus again spent much of that year around Galilee. He appointed the twelve apostles and continued healing and teaching, often with parables. Herod's murder of John the Baptist was reported to Jesus. As the year concluded, Jesus sent the apostles out "to proclaim the kingdom of God and to heal the sick" (Luke 9:2). After that, as recorded in John, Jesus returned to Jerusalem, where he healed a blind man on the Sabbath and became engaged in acrimonious discussions with the Jewish leaders.

G. The Third Year, Opposition to Jesus—Matthew 14:13-16:28; Mark 6:30-9:1; Luke 9:10-27; John 6:1-71

Back in Galilee, Jesus met his apostles after they returned from their preaching and healing mission. Opposition from the Jewish authorities increased. Toward the end of this time period, Peter confessed of Jesus, "You are the Messiah, the Son of the living God" (Matt. 16:16). After this, Jesus foretold his own death and warned his followers of the price of discipleship.

H. Last Months of Jesus' Teaching—Matthew 17:1-20:34; Mark 9:2-10:52; Luke 9:28-19:27; John 7:1-11:57

Jesus took Peter, James, and John up a high mountain and was transfigured before them as he conversed with Moses and Elijah. After that, Jesus walked back to Jerusalem for the Feast of Tabernacles and began teaching in the temple. He aroused great hostility among the Jewish religious leaders. Much teaching was given during this period including the important parables of the good Samaritan and the prodigal son, recorded by Luke. After Jesus raised his friend Lazarus from the dead, a conspiracy by the Jewish religious leaders to kill Jesus began to grow, and Jesus withdrew from public view.

I. The Days before Jesus' Arrest—Matthew 21:1-26:30; Mark 11:1-14:31; Luke 19:28-22:39; John 12:1-17:26

The events in the days before Jesus' arrest and trial were as follows:

- Saturday, Jesus went to the town of Bethany, and Mary, the sister of Lazarus, anointed Jesus with perfume.
- Sunday, Jesus entered Jerusalem and was greeted by a great crowd shouting, "Blessed is the king of Israel!" (John 12:13).
- Monday, Jesus drove merchants from the temple and began teaching.
- Tuesday, Jesus gave extensive teaching to his disciples and the public, and the authorities began planning to kill Jesus. Judas offered his services to betray Jesus.
- Wednesday, the disciples prepared an upper room for the Passover meal.
- Thursday evening, Jesus washed the disciples' feet, and they partook of the Last Supper. They left the upper room, and Jesus continued to teach them and prayed for his followers.

J. Jesus' Arrest and Trial—Matthew 26:31–27:26; Mark 14:32–15:19; Luke 22:39–23:25; John 18:1–19:16

Thursday evening, Jesus and the disciples went to the Mount of Olives, the garden of Gethsemane, where Jesus prayed,

> Father, if you are willing, take this cup from me; yet not my will but yours be done. (Luke 22:42)

Jesus was betrayed by Judas. Within about nine overnight hours, Jesus went through a series of trials before

Annas the high priest; the Sanhedrin (a tribunal of elders); Pilate, the Roman administrator; Herod; and back to Pilate again. Pilate condemned him to death, and he was led out to be crucified. During these trials, Peter denied that he knew Jesus.

K. Jesus' Crucifixion and Burial—Matthew 27:27-66; Mark 15:20-47; Luke 23:26-56; John 19:17-42

On Friday, Jesus was led to a hill outside Jerusalem named "Golgotha" and was crucified between two thieves. The Four Gospels provide a detailed account of the events of that day, culminating with Jesus' burial in a tomb, "cut in the rock" (Luke 23:53), provided by Joseph of Arimathea, a member of the Jewish Sanhedrin.

L. Jesus' Resurrection and Ascension—Matthew 28:1-20; Mark 16:1-20; Luke 24:1-53; John 20:1-21:25; Acts 1:1-11

On Sunday, the first day of the week, the women who followed Jesus, including Mary, found the stone rolled away from the entrance to the tomb, and Peter and John came to find the tomb empty. Jesus appeared to Mary and others, and on the next Sunday, he appeared to ten of the disciples, excluding Thomas. A week later Jesus appeared again to the disciples, this time with Thomas. Jesus appeared again to some of the disciples, including Peter, while they were fishing, and Jesus reinstated Peter.

Some days later, it is reported, Jesus ascended into heaven. The most detailed description is provided by Luke at the beginning of the book of Acts. Jesus' last words were,

> But you will receive power when the Holy Spirit comes on you; and you will be my witnesses in Jerusalem, and in all Judea and Samaria, and to the ends of the earth. (Acts 1:8)

After Jesus' Ascension: The Eyewitness Accounts of Jesus' Life and Resurrection by the Apostle Peter and Other Jesus' Followers. (Acts 2:14-40; 10:1-48)

In the book of Acts, Luke's second book, he records the events of the Christian community for about thirty years after Jesus' resurrection. In his gospel, his first book, Luke drew material from those who were eyewitnesses. His ability to accomplish this becomes clear because Luke travelled with the apostle Paul and met apostles such as James and Peter and others who knew Jesus personally.

Luke records the apostle Peter's first eyewitness summary of the life of Jesus, given in a sermon within weeks of Jesus' resurrection.

> Fellow Israelites, listen to this: Jesus of Nazareth was a man accredited by God to you by miracles, wonders and signs, which God did among you through him, as you yourselves know. This man was handed over to you by God's deliberate plan and foreknowledge; and you, with the help of wicked men, put him to death by nailing him to the cross. But God raised him from the dead, freeing him from the agony of death, because it was impossible for death to keep its hold on him. (Acts 2:22-24)

Peter's second summary of Jesus' life was given some years later, when Peter was sent by God to witness to Cornelius, a Roman centurion.

You know the message God sent to the people of Israel, announcing the good news of peace through Jesus Christ, who is Lord of all. You know what has happened throughout the province of Judea, beginning in Galilee after the baptism that John preached—how God anointed Jesus of Nazareth with the Holy Spirit and power, and how he went around doing good and healing all who were under the power of the devil, because God was with him.

We are witnesses of everything he did in the country of the Jews and in Jerusalem. They killed him by hanging him on a cross, but God raised him from the dead on the third day and caused him to be seen. He was not seen by all the people, but by witnesses whom God had already chosen—by us who ate and drank with him after he rose from the dead. He commanded us to preach to the people and to testify that he is the one whom God appointed as judge of the living and the dead. All the prophets testify about him *that everyone who believes in him receives forgiveness of sins through his name.* (Acts 10:36–43)

Appendix 3

The Ten Commandments

And God spoke all these words:

I am the Lord your God, who brought you out of Egypt, out of the land of slavery.

You shall have no other gods before me.

You shall not make for yourself an image in the form of anything in heaven above or on the earth beneath or in the waters below. You shall not bow down to them or worship them; for I, the Lord your God, am a jealous God, punishing the children for the sin of the parents to the third and fourth generation of those who hate me, but showing love to a thousand generations of those who love me and keep my commandments.

You shall not misuse the name of the Lord your God, for the Lord will not hold anyone guiltless who misuses his name.

Remember the Sabbath day by keeping it holy. Six days you shall labor and do all your work, but the seventh day is a sabbath to the Lord your God. On it you shall not do any work, neither you, nor your son or daughter, nor your male or female servant, nor your animals, nor any foreigner residing in your towns. For in six days the Lord made the heavens and the earth, the sea, and all that is in them, but he rested on the seventh day. Therefore, the Lord blessed the Sabbath day and made it holy.

Honor your father and your mother, so that you may live long in the land the Lord your God is giving you.

You shall not murder.

You shall not commit adultery.

You shall not steal.

You shall not give false testimony against your neighbor.

You shall not covet your neighbor's house. You shall not covet your neighbor's wife, or his male or female servant, his ox or donkey, or anything that belongs to your neighbor.

(Exodus 20:1–17)

References and Notes

1. Alasdair MacIntyre, *After Virtue: A Study in Moral Theory* (Notre Dame, IN: University of Notre Dame Press, 1981), 216.

2. Richard Gelwick, *The Way of Discovery: An Introduction to the Thought of Michael Polanyi* (Oxford: Oxford University Press, 1977) 111–12.

3. For an excellent telling of the story from an agnostic perspective, see Tom Holland, *Dominion: How the Christian Revolution Remade the World* (New York: Basic Books, 2021).

4. *Catechism of Catholic Church*, 2nd ed. (Washington, DC: United States Catholic Conference, 2000), para. 2761, quoting Tertullian.

5. Darrell W. Johnson, *Fifty-Seven Words That Changed the World: A Journey Through the Lord's Prayer* (Vancouver, BC: Regent College, 2005).

6. See N. T. Wright and Michael F. Bird, *The New Testament in Its World* (Grand Rapids: Zondervan Academic, 2019).

7. Christopher Hitchens, Richard Dawkins, Sam Harris, and Daniel Dennett, *The Four Horsemen: The Conversation That Sparked an Atheist Revolution* (New York: Random House, 2019).

8. Peter Medawar, *The Limit of Science* (Oxford: Oxford University Press, 1954), 66–67.

9. Hitchens et al., *Four Horsemen*, 24.

10. Blaise Pascal, *Pascal's Pensées* (New York: E. P. Dutton, 1958), 513, #140.

11. Justo Gonzales, *Teach Us to Pray* (Grand Rapids: Eerdmans, 2020), 1128. Kindle.

12. Glenn Tinder, *The Political Meaning of Christianity: The Prophetic Stance; An Interpretation* (San Francisco: HarperCollins, 1991), 74.

13. John R. W. Stott, *Christian Counter Culture* (Leicester, UK: Inter-Varsity, 1978), 147–48.

14. See Rodney Stark, *The Rise of Christianity: How the Obscure, Marginal Jesus Movement Became the Dominant Religious Force in the Western World in a Few Centuries* (San Francisco: Harper Collins, 1997).

15. Merriam-Webster, s.v. "guilt," accessed May 23, 2023, https://unabridged.merriam-webster.com/collegiate/guilt.

16. A picture of Kant's tombstone at the Columbia College website: https://www.college.columbia.edu/core/content/kant%E2%80%99s-tombstone-kaliningrad.

17. Johnson, *Fifty-Seven Words*, 86.

18. Alexander Maclaren, "Forgive Us Our Debts," Biblehub, accessed May 1, 2022, https://biblehub.com/sermons/auth/maclaren/forgive_us_our_debts'.htm.

19. Stott, *Christian Counter Culture*, 250.

20. N. T. Wright, "Christianity Offers No Answers about the Coronavirus, It's Not Supposed To," *Time*, March 29, 2020, https://time.com/5808495/coronavirus-christianity/vc.

21. Harry Lee Poe, *Becoming C. S. Lewis: A Biography of Young Jack Lewis (1898–1918)* (Wheaton, IL: Crossway, 2019), 274.

22. Flavius Josephus referred to Jesus in his *Antiquities of the Jews* written around 93–94 CE, and the Roman historian Tacitus referred to the crucifixion of Christ in his *Annals* around 116 CE.

23. D. E. Isom, *The Walk with the Word: Parallel Gospels* (Redlands, CA: Walk with the Word, 2018).

24. Wright and Bird, *New Testament in Its World*.

www.ingramcontent.com/pod-product-compliance
Lightning Source LLC
Chambersburg PA
CBHW060531080526
44586CB00012B/696